For Jeff

With my Best Wishes

for your future

MSgt Dave Puckett

9 Apr 96

MEMORIES

MSG David H. Puckett (Ret.)

VANTAGE PRESS
New York / Atlanta
Los Angeles / Chicago

FIRST EDITION

Published by Vantage Press, Inc.
516 West 34th Street, New York, New York 10001

Manufactured in the United States of America
ISBN: 0-533-07308-1
Library of Congress Catalog Card No.: 86-91500

To the more than fifty-thousand Americans who gave their all in Vietnam and to the thousands who served honorably and returned to a divided, ungrateful nation, only to discover after twenty years the battles are still being fought in their minds

CONTENTS

AUTHOR'S NOTE

The title of this book says it all. It is a personal reflection of what I saw and felt in Vietnam.

This is not a novel or historical chronology of the war, nor is it meant to be. It is a random collection of my personal memories and thoughts during that period of my life, which will remain with me forever.

The events are all true and took place during my first tour of duty in Vietnam with the Big Red One. All the characters are real people. With the exception of a few well-known personalities, their names have been changed to protect their identity and well-deserved privacy.

For any terms or remarks that I use in this book, such as "grunt," "gook," or profanity that may upset some people, I would like to offer apologies now. I use the terms because they reflect the true accepted terms of that period. I surely respect the grunts because I was one for so long.

I had every intention of writing this book shortly after returning to the "world" in 1967, but someone "relieved" me of my diary and pictures during a check prior to my return. My duties in the army, including another tour with the Big Red One, did not allow me the time needed to write the book.

Every article or book I read on Vietnam seemed to

dwell on and stress the bad points of the conflict. The GIs that served were continually referred to as "pot smoking," "officer-fragging" and "mutiny-minded" soldiers who were somehow responsible for the outcome of the war. These remarks did not describe the soldiers or units I served with.

I felt it was my responsibility, just as it was my responsibility to protect my troops in combat, to truthfully relate my memories and experiences during this difficult period in our history.

The soldiers I served with, probably the best the U.S. has ever fielded in history, were not only good but they were human, too. In some small way, I hope I have managed to show that one fact.

FOREWORD

If you have taken this book in hand to explore another strategic analysis of Vietnam from 1940 onward or to consider once again the philosophical explanations of the campus riots and traitorous exodus to Canada, then put it down. *Memories* is just that, the recording in a superb, readable, and down-to-earth manner of the battlefield experiences of a combat leader. MSG David Puckett was a regular army NCO who did his duty in the time-honored tradition of our infantry NCO corps. Those readers who have walked in his boots need no further explanation.

The description of arriving in Saigon aboard a charter jet transport will bring back memories to all who served in that combat zone. The progression on down to the rifle company narrows the memory lane to those grunts whose fate it was to travel that road. The perspective of Vietnam differs as to your view of those eventful days. Mine, as an infantry battalion commander (3/7 Infantry 199th Light Infantry Brigade, '67–68) is somewhat different from MSG Puckett's, yet in so many ways, these memories are similar and today weld that everlasting bond between those who proudly wear the Combat Infantry Badge.

Early on, the author states that he does not intend to labor in the political considerations of that war and with one exception does not. I commend him, for that is no easy task to follow when reflecting on Vietnam. His description of the adventures experienced by platoon members during their "off duty" trips to the ville will bring a smile to the lips of many, just as the loss of a comrade during a fire fight will bring tears to your eyes.

The reader will find the chronology of *Memories* easy reading with the side excursions well done and selected to reinforce the flow. In addition, deserving credit is given to those supporting forces such as Army Aviation, Field Artillery, and Tactical Air for their timely and vital assistance without which many of us would not be here today. Once again, the position of the "grunt" in the master scheme of things is confirmed. No one has yet found a substitute for the rifleman who must fight for and occupy the terrain of his enemy. All others are in support of this ultimate weapon.

Today, many years later, Vietnam veterans have finally been accorded some degree of public recognition by the nation. There are those who say we lost the war—I would argue that point in concert with many others. But it will be for history to render the final judgment. *Memories* is a must for your reading list and library. I commend MSG David Puckett for his bringing forth this sobering reflection on those times. I am proud to have had the privilege to participate in this effort. To do so has opened doors to thoughts, times, and emotions long since past.

John K. Gibler
Colonel, Infantry
U.S. Army (Retired)

INTRODUCTION

Two decades ago, David Puckett and I served as fellow soldiers in the Republic of South Vietnam, that oppressed country some 10,000 miles from "home." Both Blue Spaders in the Big Red One (26th Infantry in the 1st Infantry Divison) we fought together in the battle of AP GU exactly 20 years ago, one of the largest and most vicious fought by Americans in that war, which today looms large in our memories.

Memories, written after that first combat tour of David's 1966–1967, is dedicated to "the more than 50,000 Americans" who died there, and to the many more who "served honorably and returned to a divided and ungrateful nation. . . . " Unique in his approach, however, is that he has left politics and domestic disturbances here in America to others. With clarity and candor, he has devoted his talents to recapture those "battles . . . still being fought in . . . [the] . . . minds" of those who served and returned.

Recalled clearly are those emotions of soldiers in combat: the elations and depressions, the humor and tears, the respect for a fellow professional who fights bravely at his side and the disdain for the shirker and coward. Above all, this fine soldier reflects pride in those whom he led and in his own senior non-commissioned and commissioned leaders. His country placed him there to perform his duty, and he did it.

xiii

Through the art of his pen, we smelled and felt the jungle and its "stifling heat," had compassion for the fear: "the sweaty palms, the dry mouth, and the . . . rapid . . . heartbeat . . . "; and understood "the bond that develops between men engaged in combat. . . . " That bond, which he compares to the family, drew together that small group of soldiers with whom he served—men of different race, age, and background—as they worked and played, ate and drank, slept and fought at day and night, and lived or died. That "strong bond, almost like love" is what he remembers and what we share.

David Puckett saw clearly the horrors, the harsh side of war. Yet we know that his professionalism and response to his nation's call prevailed, as he returned voluntarily in 1969 to serve again with the Big Red One. When the Division returned to Kansas the next year, he helped bring the colors home.

My reflections while reading this excellent book confirm the author's message: "These memories are forever."

ALEXANDER M. HAIG, JR.

McLean, Virginia
April 1, 1987

PROLOGUE

OCTOBER 1967. It was a beautiful bright fall morning in Montgomery, Alabama. The sky was cloudless; a gentle breeze lifted the flag over City Hall but failed to disturb the pigeons, busy with their endless courting atop the old majestic structure. It was only eight thirty in the morning and my newly purchased suit and tie already promised an uncomfortable tenure in the cramped, stuffy meeting room of the Montgomery City Council.

As I took a seat in one of the straight-back chairs in the back of the room, I saw that I wasn't the only one who seemed uncomfortable and a little out of place. About twenty-five or thirty other young men with close-cropped hair and somewhat ill-fitting new clothes were fidgeting in the smoke-filled room. The mayor had just started his comments.

"Ladies and gentlemen, it gives me great pleasure this morning to officially welcome some very distinguished Americans, and citizens of Montgomery, back to our fair city and this great country of ours."

After the expected amount of nervous throat clearing and rearranging of chairs, the mayor continued.

"We have asked you here this morning to present each of you with a small token, which represents your city's congratulations and, most of all, appreciation, for

1

your recently completed meritorious service to your country in the Republic of Vietnam."

The small room was momentarily filled with a smattering of polite applause by the other city officials in attendance. The mayor asked each individual to come forward as his name was called to receive the small parchment scroll.

"Sergeant Gary Smothers, U.S. Army . . . " There was an awkward silence as a young tall black, wearing a green beret of the elite Special Forces, made his way up the aisle with the aid of his still alienlike crutches, accepted the scroll, and made his way proudly back to his seat.

My name was called toward the end of the presentation, and I'm afraid I missed the closing remarks by the mayor, as my attention must have been directed to the small scroll. At the top of the scroll was a picture of the American flag. Underneath was a piece credited to William Tyler Page, titled "The American's Creed." At the bottom of the scroll it read " . . . Presented to Sergeant First Class David H. Puckett . . . with congratulations and appreciation for meritorious service to your country. Your patriotism is symbolic of the highest ideals of American citizenship." It was signed by an Alabama congressman.

My thoughts were brought back to the little room by the applause and shuffling of chairs as the back slapping, hand-shaking, and offerings of congratulations signified the end of the ceremony.

The gentle breeze that touched my face as we walked down the steps was welcome relief after being in the stuffy meeting room. After a few handshakes and wishes of good luck, the small gathering began to disperse and go their separate ways. At that moment a loud crash echoed off the buildings, and I heard myself screaming, "Get down! Get down!" as I dove to the sidewalk. Only a few seconds had elapsed when I realized that the loud crash had only been a car backfiring and not the expected crash of a Viet Cong mortar or rocket. Embarrassed, I quickly got to my feet, walked over to the tall black NCO, picked up his crutches, and helped him up.

"I'm sorry, man. You okay?"

"Yeah. No sweat. Thanks."

It was then that I noticed the pedestrians and the people in the cars who had stopped and were staring in disbelief at this strange spectacle of young men, some in civilian clothing and some in uniform, picking themselves up from the sidewalk. There were whispers and some slow head shaking among the spectators as they continued on their way.

Aside from wishing I could run and jump in a hole, I wished I could find the words to explain my actions and those of my comrades to these unknowing citizens; but what could I say?

"Sorry folks . . . just some . . . memories."

Chapter 1

WELCOME TO SUNNY VIETNAM

OCTOBER 13, 1966. All the joking, gaiety, and false bravado aboard the Pan Am jet suddenly came to an abrupt halt when the slightly tense voice of the captain came over the intercom.

"Ladies and gentlemen, if you'll please find your way to your seats and kindly fasten your seatbelts, we'll see if we can set this bird down as gently as possible. We're about ten minutes out of Saigon, at 25,000 feet. Our final approach to Tan Son Nhut will be a little steep. We've found it doesn't allow Charlie too much time for target practice."

Nervous laughter, and I do mean nervous, filled the plane. I noticed our stewardess had replaced her ever-present smile with a look of grim determination as she secured her work station and prepared to buckle up.

We all wondered when we reboarded the plane after a brief stopover in Guam what happened to all the young beautiful stewardesses that started out with us in California. All of a sudden we had two men stewards and three rather older ladies to go into battle with us. I found out later that many of the airlines didn't want to risk their young beauties with a short stopover in Saigon. All the crew on this plane were older and had volunteered to be our hosts. They would also receive hazardous-duty pay for their flight and short stay in a combat zone. The plane would only be on the ground long enough to refuel and reload for the return trip back to the world.

The voice of the captain came to life once more. "We're starting our final approach at this time. You'll notice it will be a little steeper than usual, and we should be on the ground in a short time. Hang on."

He didn't really have to tell us the last part. We actually had to hang on to our seat arms when the nose of the plane dipped. My seat mate, a young SP4 from Georgia, turned his head in my direction.

"I shore hope he can level this thing out in time! I don't know which would be worse, getting shot at or crashing this sucker flat as a pancake!"

After what seemed like ten minutes of reckless falling amid the noise and vibrations of the jet, we leveled off and felt the slight jolt of wheels touching solid ground. The cheering and hooting inside the plane almost drowned out the roar of the jet engines, as they were thrown into reverse to slow us down and hopefully keep us on the runway. Praises for the captain and crew were being widely voiced. My Georgia seat mate smiled and said, "That boy knows he can fly this baby!"

As we taxied to the main terminal area, all eyes were glued to the windows. The entire airport had been converted to a combat airfield. Sandbagged U-shaped revetments covered the surrounding runways and taxi ramps. Ground crews were busy loading bombs and rearming the sleek camouflaged jets parked inside the revetments. Every visible runway was active with planes of every description taking off or coming in.

"This place makes JFK look tame," remarked an air force captain in front of me. One week later he would probably be flying a small L-19 observation plane from this base, directing fast movers to a target in support of an infantry unit in contact.

As we pulled up to the terminal, the voice of the captain came over the intercom. "We'll be unloading in about three minutes. The temperature in beautiful downtown Saigon is 110 degrees. On behalf of the crew and myself, we hope you have a safe tour and sincerely hope to see each and every one of you in about one year."

Our plane was boarded by two REMFs (The grunts' nice description for someone with a soft rear echelon job) who quickly gave us instructions on where to pick up our luggage and where to find the different processing stations within the terminal.

Even with the forewarning from the captain and all the classes back in the states, there was no way to prepare for the tropic heat that greeted us as we got off the plane. My starched khakis were damp and sticky by the time I walked down the boarding ladder. There was no breeze, and I was sure the tower had made a mistake when they gave the temperature to the captain.

"I don't see how anybody can operate in this heat!" I remarked.

"Me neither, man, and I thought it was hot in Georgia!"

★   ★   ★   ★

"Welcome to South-Fuckin' Vietnam!" Shouted welcomes greeted us from a file of jungle-fatigue-clad GIs passing us to board the plane we had just left.

"How's the world doin'?"

"Good luck, green weenies! You're gonna need it!"

"I'd shoot myself if I had a year left in this hellhole!"

6

Our file shot back appropriate remarks, and the bantering continued until we had entered the terminal building. I was sure there would be relief from the heat once inside the terminal. Wrong. The old, heavily taxed ceiling fans did little or nothing to cool the over-crowded terminal. There must have been 800 Vietnamese and servicemen, elbow to elbow, seemingly trying to get to the same place.

"Hey sarge, has Saigon fell and nobody told us?" I asked an MP at the baggage area.

"Nah. Just a typical day at Saigon International," was the reply. "The smart gooks are trying to get the hell out of here!"

We were loaded on an OD bus for transportation to Long Binh where we would be processed for final shipment to our units. The windows of the bus thankfully were down, but they were covered by a thick wire mesh.

"Now that they've got us here, they sure as hell ain't going to let us get away!" remarked one of the soldiers.

The armed MP in the bus explained the wire mesh to us.

"The wire is over the windows for your protection. We don't want one of Uncle Ho's disciples to lob a grenade in to welcome you. It's hot enough on this bus already. It's about ten miles to LBJ ranch but we'll be going through some narrow streets on the way. If the bus should suddenly speed up, just duck your heads and hang on. Don't try to sightsee. You'll have time for an R and R later."

The circulating air, even though it was hot, was welcome as the driver pulled away from the terminal. I lit up a cigarette and watched the old, almost antique, AT-6 single-engine planes of the Vietnamese Air Force as we passed their headquarters. The tiny streets were packed with bicycles, small Honda motor bikes and Vietnamese women and children seemingly oblivious to the large bus trying to make its way through the narrow streets. The whistles and hoots from the young soldiers on the bus drew shy glances from the young delicate Vietnamese girls dressed in their sheer long dresses. Young children with outstretched hands were pleading, "Hey, you GI! You give me cigarette!" We laughed at their reply when no cigarettes were thrown from the cage windows.

"Fuck you! You numba 10 GI!"

"Just like back home on the block!" a young private remarked.

With the exception of all the activity and the camouflaged jets at the airport, Saigon looked like it was business as usual. War seemed to be someone else's problem far away, surely not these people's in the city. My thoughts went back to what the MP had said and I wondered . . . *What kind of a war is this if we can't even secure a ten-mile strip between our airport and the largest base we had in this country?* I would understand why in a very short while.

★   ★   ★   ★

WELCOME TO LBJ RANCH,
HQ, USARV,
WE SERVE, LONG BINH, RVN

read the big sign arched over the entrance to the sprawling complex. Long, one- and two-story tropical buildings dotted the large base as far as you could see. Long Binh served as the in and out processing point for all army personnel and housed the headquarters for many service and support elements in Vietnam.

All the tropical hootches were sandbagged up to about four feet on the outside. Not much protection from a direct hit by a rocket or mortar, but at least it provided a sense of false security. The only other things that would hint we were in a war zone were the long sandbagged rocket and mortar shelters that were located randomly around the processing point. They were constructed by digging a narrow trench wide enough and long enough to hold about fifteen or twenty personnel. This trench was covered by half a section of a metal culvert and then covered by three or four layers of sandbags.

The processing point was a complete city in itself. There were tropical hootches of varying sizes for everything. In addition to the barracks for the new and departing personnel, there were two mess halls; officer, NCO and enlisted clubs; a small PX; a barber shop; a laundry (for the permanent party personnel); and latrines located around the outer edges of the little city. It was these small four- and five-seaters that produced the unforgettable aroma of all base camps in Vietnam! Body waste was collected in fifty-five-gallon drums that had been cut in half and placed beneath the cut out seats of the latrine. Each morning these drums were removed, filled with diesel fuel and burnt. The resultant smell became a permanent part of the entire base area. I thought to myself, that job had to be the epitome of the term "shit detail!"

We were all processed in typical army fashion—hurry up and wait. We stood in line to process our orders; we stood in line at the legal office to process a will or power of attorney; we stood in line to trade in our greenbacks for funny money (MPC); we stood in line to receive our partial issue of jungle fatigues; we stood in line at the mess hall; and, yes, we even stood in line waiting for one of the holes of the four-seater to be vacated.

I had more trouble getting to sleep that first night in country than I had imagined possible. Even though the barracks had large fans at each end, it was still hot. Just moments after laying down on the bunk, the sheets felt wet and sticky. The butterflies in my stomach didn't help matters either. The excitement and suspense (and yes, fear) of the unknown began to seek a place in my thoughts. We would be getting our assignments and transportation to our units first thing in the morning, and this war, in this seemingly peaceful setting, started to become more of a reality to me.

A portion of the distant black sky took on an eerie glow as artillery illumination rounds lit up the battlefield for some unit in contact. The barely audible sounds of explosions brought the reality closer.

"Hey Robinson, look! Way out there. Somebody's catching hell," I said.

"Yeah. I hope we're on the giving end and not the receiving," replied the staff sergeant in the bunk next to mine.

The flares and crumps of artillery lasted about fifteen minutes. As I dozed off, my thoughts once again focused on this strange war. Somewhere out there in the jungle a unit was fighting for their lives, while I slept on clean, white sheets.

★ ★ ★ ★

The next morning my name, along with about thirty-five others, was called to report, bag and baggage, for transportation to Di An, the basecamp of the 1st Infantry Division.

After throwing our bags on one of the three deuce and a half trucks, we each were issued an M14 rifle by division liaison personnel. We were then instructed to load up on the remaining empty trucks. Each truck had a lieutenant in the cab as vehicle commander. Our small convoy was to be escorted by two MP gun jeeps.

A young private seated across from me asked, "Hey Sarge, what are we supposed to do with these guns? I think they forgot to give us some bullets!"

I repeated the question to the young lieutenant in the cab of our truck.

"Oh, don't sweat it. They're just for looks. We've only got about fifteen miles to go and the road is secure."

I walked back to my seat. "The LT said don't sweat it, Jones," I reassured the private. "Just make like Hank Aaron and swing away if anything happens!"

"No shit!" came the reply. "I can see the headlines now . . . The Congressional Medal of Honor was awarded to PVT Jones today when he knocked the heads off five VC with an empty M14!"

As if in response to our shouts and laughter, the MP from the lead gun jeep walked up to our truck. "Listen up. We'll be moving out in about zero five. In case the convoy speeds up, get down on the bed and stay put until we slow down. We've only lost one truck in six months."

"He could have gone all day without saying that last bit of information," remarked the SSG sitting next to me.

"Amen."

With his short briefing complete, the MP returned to the lead jeep, and we were off to Di An.

Chapter 2

IT DON'T MEAN NOTHIN'

THE TRIP TO DI AN WAS, THANK GOD, PEACEFUL. Small villages and farmland dotted the lush green countryside. The rural areas were dedicated to rice farming. The rice paddies were laid out in squares or rectangles, with dikes surrounding the flooded paddies. Row after row of hand-planted green rice shoots covered the area. The workers, all older men and women, wore black silk pants and shirts and big straw conical hats. The younger children were in charge of the only machinery used in the paddies, the big lumbering water buffalo. The kids seemed to have complete control over the mean-looking animals with nothing but a long slender stick. With the exception of a few scattered shell-pocked buildings, the scenery was that of calm and serenity.

The more enterprising children had opened "car washes" along the banks of rivers and streams, complete with a tin-covered lean-to that advertised cold Cokes and beer. Names like "USA Car Wash" and "American Truck Wash" adorned the shacks. Military vehicles of all types, jeeps to tanker transports, could be seen lined up waiting their turn while the drivers had a "cool one" in their hand and, normally, a young Vietnamese girl on their lap.

All of these first impressions of business as usual in this seemingly placid country made it hard to believe that we had made this long trip to help these people fight for and save their country. We seemed to be more concerned about the outcome of this war than they did.

★ ★ ★ ★

A large fence, fronted by three rows of concertina wire, ran from a sandbagged military police bunker that served as the entrance to Di An. WELCOME TO THE HOME OF THE BIG RED ONE, the arched sign over the road greeted us. A large billboard-type sign across the road from the MP sentry bunker adorned with the division patch and unit emblems, expounded the famous division's motto:

NO MISSION TOO DIFFICULT

NO SACRIFICE TOO GREAT

DUTY FIRST

The division's basecamp was a smaller, scaled-down version of Long Binh. All the division's service and support units were based here. Our destination, the replacement company, was about two hundred yards from the MP gate. The close proximity of the large bunkers on the perimeter to the tropical hootches of the replacement company brought the reality of war a little closer to home. One other event that made me aware of the current situation was being issued a real M16 rifle for our "convoy M14s." This was done immediately after unloading and dropping our bags on a bunk in one of the hootches.

After a decent meal in the mess hall, we spent the remainder of the day processing. Our 201 file was dropped off at the personnel hootch, and then it was on to finance, where we got our travel pay and any other pay that might be due. Allotments were made to wives and mothers back home. Money would not be such a necessity over here, where most of our time would be spent in the jungle. Things were so cheap in the PX that you really didn't need a lot of money, even for necessities such as shaving cream, razor blades, and so forth. The opportunities to get to a nice PX like the REMFs had in Saigon or Long Binh were few and far between. I did manage to buy a Seiko watch during a "trading" trip to a Navy base near Saigon. I still have the watch to this day. It not only keeps perfect time but also brings back many memories, both good and bad.

Some items that we surely didn't need to buy for our everyday jungle hygiene were after-shave lotion, deodorant, or nice-smelling soap. My radio man taught me a basic survival lesson prior to my first S & D (search and destroy) patrol. I had just finished shaving and was about to drown my face in English Leather after-shave.

"Sarge, you put that stuff on and you better find yourself another RTO. You'll smell like a rolling French whorehouse! Every gook in the AO will know where we are, and I don't want to be nowhere near you. I might catch a ricochet!"

I thought he might be kidding me at first, but he assured me he was "serious as an L-shaped ambush."

"He's right, Sarge," one of my squad leaders said. "Mr. Charles can smell us already without us wearing all that nice-smelling stuff."

A veteran of the platoon, a twenty-year-old buck sergeant who had been with the platoon for ten months since his arrival as a PFC, swore that he could smell the VC. He later made me into a believer.

14

Cigarettes and tobacco were dirt cheap in the PX, which led to much small-scale illegal black market activities with the Vietnamese. The locals were crazy about menthol cigarettes, especially "Saleem." Expensive 35mm cameras could be bought for one-third the stateside price. Nice three-piece tailor-made silk suits could be had for about $50.00.

I saved more money in this twelve-month period than I have managed in all the years since.

The replacement company also served as the out-processing point for all division personnel rotating back to the world. It also served as a stopover place for departing and returning from R & R (Rest and Recuperation). To be eligible for an R & R you had to be in-country for six months. You could choose from about six locations to spend five days in another world away from the everyday strains of search and destroy and incoming mortars and rockets. It was a chance to go to either Hawaii, Bangkok, Hong Kong, Taipei, or Australia; sleep in an air-conditioned room with a real bed and clean sheets. An opportunity to let out pent-up emotions and spend an intimate few days with a member of the opposite sex. Most of the "old timers" had another acronym for this time, I & I, which stood for intoxication and intercourse. Most of the married guys went to Hawaii, since they could meet the wife and have a second honeymoon. The single, younger guys didn't care; they just wanted to get away for a while.

My second night in country was much like the first night in that I didn't get much sleep again. The heat and humidity only seemed to grow more intense. About the time I would doze off, a few drunks would stumble in. The ones going on R & R were the ones likely to raise more hell. They had temporarily escaped the jungle and were intent on making the most of it. The ones going back to the world after their time in the boonies were more calm and collected. They just wanted to get a good, safe night's rest and get on the "Freedom Bird." Their celebration would come later when they were far away from the jungles and these hootches.

"Man, I got a load to drop when I get to Hong Kong! Those broads better be resting up now, 'cause when the Boss hits town, it's gonna be party time for five days and nights!"

"Tell it like it is!"

"You guys knock it off," remarked an irritated voice out of the dark, "some folks are trying to sleep in here."

The hootch grew quiet once again after the celebrants tripped and stumbled to their bunks. Through the chorus of snoring and the drone of mosquitoes, sleep finally came. It seemed hard to believe that in a short time I would be able to sleep at the drop of a hat, even through a rocket attack.

The next morning after breakfast all the new arrivals were gathered in the dayroom for a briefing by a division information officer. The division units were posted on a big map, allowing us to see the entire area of operations. The young lieutenant gave us a short briefing on recent and current operations of all three brigades. Most of the units had been involved in major operations in the past month with light contact and favorable results for the division. A long list of enemy equipment, supplies, and personnel that had been captured or destroyed was posted for our information. No mention of division personnel or equipment losses were made. I wondered if we were getting a true picture of the situation. The lieutenant closed by stating most of the activity now was local patrols and search and destroy missions.

After another hour of informal briefings, about ten men, along with myself, were trucked to the helipad to await transportation to our unit basecamp. I was being assigned to the 1st Battalion 26th Infantry of the 1st Brigade. The brigade basecamp was located at Phuoc Vinh, about thirty miles north of Di An, as the crow flies. I was glad we were going by chopper and not on a truck, but I was still puzzled. We had been issued an M16 here at Di An, along with jungle fatigues and a steel helmet; but we still were not issued ammunition! The helicopter might be a little safer, but what were we supposed to do if the chopper was shot down?

We logged in at the heliport and were told to make ourselves comfortable and that we would be called when a chopper was going our way. The first chopper came in about thirty-five minutes after we arrived, but its destination was Lai Khe. A young PFC, returning from R & R, had rode over with us from the replacement company. I had overheard part of a conversation he had with one of the new arrivals, and I knew he was trying to get to Lai Khe. He had sprawled out on one of the benches inside the hootch and apparently had gone to sleep. I walked over and shook him. "This chopper's going to Lai Khe. Isn't that where you're headed?"

"Yeah," he replied as he turned back over and got comfortable again, "but I ain't in no hurry to get back. If I sleep a little longer maybe I'll miss the last bird back."

"But won't you get in trouble?" I asked. It was at this time that I heard two of the most commonly used phrases by the "grunts" in Vietnam.

"It don't mean nothin'. What they gonna do—send me to Vietnam?"

Chapter 3

BASECAMP AND JUNGLE SCHOOL

FOR THE FIRST TIME IN THREE DAYS I WAS COOL. I wish I could have found a way to bottle the feeling. My ride to Phuoc Vinh turned out to be a huey slick with the doors removed. Zipping along at eighty knots, 1,500 feet up was, I decided, the way to go. The vibrations and noise of the rotor blades was made bearable by the cool air flowing through the cabin. One of the door gunners tapped me on the shoulder and motioned that I should roll my sleeves down. I later found this was a safety precaution, not a comfort measure. After pulling survivors from a downed huey, I saw what the fuel could do to unprotected flesh: It wasn't necessary for the fuel to be ignited to cause severe skin burns.

The mail courier who got on the chopper with me had already propped himself on his big mail sack and somehow managed to go to sleep. It didn't seem possible to me that anyone could sleep on this noisy machine as it vibrated through the air. I remember many catnaps aboard a slick now, some being the most restful sleep I'd had in days.

I noticed both door gunners, along with the pilot and aircraft commander, were making use of a lesson learned. Besides wearing a flak vest, they were also sitting on one.

I wondered if that had always been standard procedure or if someone had paid a rather painful price for that piece of wisdom.

I slid along the canvas seat to the right side of the chopper to do some sightseeing. We seemed to be following a well-defined road that looked almost orange as it sliced through the lush green of the countryside. Both sides of the road had been cleared of all vegetation for two or three hundred meters along some stretches. The engineers, using bulldozers equipped with large scraper blades, were still busy clearing the thick vegetation along the road heading north. I was to learn later that this was the infamous "Thunder Road," Highway 13. Away from the road-clearing operation, the green landscape was pock-marked with the almost perfect circles of light-orange bomb craters. The bottoms of the older craters were filled with green, stagnant water, making them stand out from the others. Clusters of small shacks dotted the panoramic view, their tin roofs reflecting the sun's brightness. Tiny, almost antlike shapes moved in the fields and rice paddies oblivious to our presence above. A huge cloud was dumping sheets of rain on one little portion of the horizon off to our right. I would soon grow to both welcome and dread these drenching rains.

We were approaching a sprawling sand-colored area carved out of the jungle. My initial thoughts that this might be Phuoc Vinh were proved wrong as our huey maintained its altitude and heading to the north. Remembering the briefing map at Di An, I realized this dot of civilization in the jungle had to be Lai Khe. A formation of seven or eight hueys heading south passed near our chopper as I began to imagine what Phuoc Vinh would be like.

★ ★ ★ ★

I could understand why Phuoc Vinh was called the division's "outpost" as we neared our destination. I'm sure the basecamp came by its name because it was the northernmost element of the division; but I had visions of other reasons as well. The air strip and helipad area were blanketed by a thick cloud of red dust. There were only a few permanent hootches with tin roofs visible. Most had canvas for tops. After seeing the large permanent-like complexes at Long Binh and Di An, the difference was like daylight and dark.

It was impossible for me to even think that in the months to come I would be glad to see this place, even for a short period of time. After days of hacking through the dense jungle and living on a constant high achieved through fear of the unknown, with the possibility of death at your next step, Phuoc Vinh seemed like paradise when we came back. It became our "safe haven." The place where we came back to unwind, to relax and recharge ourselves for the next operation. It also served as a place for remembrance. After the relaxation period, the memories and sometimes nightmares would come back. The happier times we'd had together; the feelings of closeness we shared regardless of race, color or creed. These memories often provided the spark that recharged us for the next operation. The high would come back, and I would find myself eagerly anticipating the unknown once again.

I caught a ride on a three-quarter-ton truck to my battalion's area on the north side of the base.

"Just got to the 'Nam, Sarge?" asked the young specialist behind the wheel.

"Yeah, coupla' days ago."

"Where you from back in the world?"

20

"Alabama," I replied. "I was at Fort Benning on the mortar committee when I got orders."

"Is 'at right? I took basic at Benning. I'm from La-Grange right up the road, so it wasn't too bad. Got to go home 'bout every weekend when I didn't have any duty. I used to sneak my first sergeant some white lightin' from home, so I didn't have to worry 'bout weekend KP and guard duty." His tanned face displayed a wide grin as he turned toward me.

"What outfit you in?" I asked.

"First of the 2d. We got the ville side of the perimeter."

"How long you been here?"

"I got 28 days and a wake up," he beamed. "I beat the bush for eight months with a M60, then the old man gave me this REMF job with supply. Most of the grunt outfits in the brigade try to get you a soft job if you survive the bush for seven or eight months and don't screw up. Some of the guys get so gung-ho they won't take a rear job; they want to stay out there looking for Mr. Charles. Guy in my platoon had ten days and a wake up; got his ass blew a-way by a booby trap. Ten days!" my driver shook his head as he finished. "It just don't make no sense."

We pulled off on the side of the road next to a long, tropical hootch. The sign on the front told me this was the headquarters of the "Blue Spaders"—1st Battalion 26th Infantry.

"This is where you get off, Sarge," my driver informed me.

I thanked him for the lift and got my bags.

"No sweat," he replied as he pulled onto the road. "Don't let the little dinks get 'ya down, Sarge!"

I was met by a buck sergeant in the hootch who informed me I would be assigned to the weapons platoon of Bravo Company. After taking my orders, he pointed out the company orderly room to me.

By the time I had walked the hundred yards across the road with my two bags, my new jungle fatigues were blotted with sweat. Once again I wondered when I would ever get used to the sweltering heat of Vietnam.

The small tropical hootch that housed the company orderly room was occupied by a tall black staff sergeant.

"Drop your bags and come on in," he called to me. "It's about five degrees cooler in here out of the sun." I knew he had been in-country for a while because his faded jungle fatigues were completely dry and void of any splotches of sweat.

"Thanks. I'm Sergeant Puckett," I introduced myself as I mopped sweat from my eyes.

"Sergeant Jackson. I'm the supply sergeant. Top said you should be getting in sometime this week. The company's out on road clearing and should be back in two or three days. They been out 'bout four days now. Pull up a chair and have some Kool-Aid. 'Bout the wettest thing we got around here. Least it's cool."

We had just finished processing some paperwork when the company clerk walked into the orderly room. We were introduced and Sergeant Jackson took me to a tentlike structure right across from the rear of the orderly room.

"This is the company senior NCO hootch. You can bunk in here tonight. We'll get you some sheets and a pillow over at supply when we take care of your field gear. You'll be going over to the brigade jungle school first thing in the morning."

"You mean I've got to go through more indoctrination classes?" I asked, trying to see if there was a way I could keep from going.

22

"Well, this is a little more than the classes and briefings you had back in the world. That was stateside stuff they fed you back at Benning. This school tells you what it's really like in the 'Nam. It's run by NCOs from the brigade that have survived the bush for seven or eight months. It only lasts four or five days and you'll get a chance to zero your weapon plus, poop on booby traps, ambushes and how to counter a lot of Charlie's tricks. It won't be any book stuff like you got in the states; mostly lessons-learned types o' things. It's a brigade policy that everyone from E8 down attend it. It'll be over before you know it and the company should be in when you get back."

After we returned from the supply tent with my field gear, I looked over the company area. Aside from the mess hall, the orderly room was the only real tropical hootch in the whole company area. The rest of the structures, about eight, were tents. The flooring was nothing more than sections of palleting and the general purpose tents were supported by a frame of four-by-fours. About seventy-five yards to the rear of the line of tents was the perimeter and bunkerline. Strands of concertina wire and sandbags connected large bunkers. A tall guard tower with a large spotlight and radar was in our sector. Between the tents and the bunkerline were the latrines and showers.

I wondered how relaxed you could be while taking a crap with your back to the enemy.

★   ★   ★   ★

The four-and-a-half days spent at the jungle school was not a waste of time, as I had thought it would be. Thinking back, I realize now it was without a doubt the best course of instruction I received while in the military. It was all hands-on, live situational training. These guys were telling us tried and proven methods of bettering our chances of survival after we joined our unit.

We were exposed to many different things we would encounter in the jungle. Among these were different types of the infamous homemade VC claymores, one of the deadly products of Vietnamese ingenuity. The circular mines were made in different sizes, two of the more popular being twelve inches and twenty-four inches in diameter. The front of the mine was concave for directional aiming. The explosives were obtained from American material left behind by the well-supplied GIs or taken from dud bombs dropped by our fighter planes. The shrapnel part of the mine contained anything the VC could get their hands on, including rocks, pieces of glass and again, shrapnel from our mines and bombs. The result was deadly, and they were feared by the grunts. We were also introduced to the many types of primitive, but effective, booby traps made of bamboo. We heard the unforgettable sound of the AK-47 rifle fired over our heads so we would know what it sounded like before it was too late. We saw the organization of a typical guerrilla unit and how they fought. We learned how to walk in the dense jungles and the cleared rubber plantations. We actually participated in a night ambush outside the perimeter.

The course was so good that it was over before I knew it. I gained the confidence I needed to survive in the jungle and do a good job in my unit.

One other good thing about the course (that made me feel better, anyway)—they finally gave us some live ammunition!

Chapter 4

THE MEN

THE BATTALION WAS BACK IN AND THE AREA WAS ALIVE with activity. Once again I found myself, bag and baggage, in front of the orderly room waiting to see the first sergeant and company commander.

Jungle fatigues were not made for you to look good in and allow you to project a professional, soldierly image. They were made to be practical in a tropical climate. They were, by design, loose fitting and sloppy looking.

The short man who got up from his desk to greet me as I walked in couldn't have looked more professional in his set of tailored dress greens. First Sergeant Jerry Webb was about five foot eight or nine. His starched jungle fatigues looked to be custom fitted. I noticed the coveted CIB (Combat Infantryman Badge) with the star between the wreath worn above his left pocket, which attested to the fact he had been under hostile fire in two conflicts. I introduced myself.

"Glad to have you with us, Puckett," replied the 1SG. "Let's walk up to the mess hall and grab a cup of coffee."

"Sounds good to me," I replied.

"Johnson," the 1SG called to a SP4 sitting behind a dusty typewriter, "if anybody's looking for me, I'll be in the mess hall with Sergeant Puckett."

"Okay, Top," replied the clerk.

We passed the mortar platoon area on the way to the

25

mess hall. About eight or nine guys were busy cleaning and oiling a couple of the eighty-ones.

"You guys better get your T-shirts on," remarked the first sergeant as we walked past the men. "You're getting a new section sergeant today. I'd hate for him to think you were a bunch of bums." He smiled at me and winked.

"Sure thing, Top," came the reply as we continued on to the mess hall.

The mess hall was relatively cool as we sat down at a table with our coffee. After giving the 1SG a brief rundown on my previous assignments and qualifications, he began to fill me in on the company and my platoon.

"I've been in this man's army almost twenty years, Puckett," he began. "I've seen a lot of good units and bad units in that time. I was a squad leader in the 3rd Infantry during the Korean conflict. I've held every job there is in an infantry unit, all the way from recruit to company commander." He paused and took a swallow of his coffee.

"I've been the first sergeant of this outfit for six months. It's a good company; best in the battalion. I'd even go as far as to say the best in the brigade. Our casualty rate is low, and we always get the job done. The company commander is a young first lieutenant due to make captain in a few months. He's been the CO for almost a year, and he just extended. He takes care of the troops, and he's coolheaded under fire. You'll like the way he operates."

First Sergeant Webb took a sip of coffee and lit up a cigarette.

"Now for the bad news," he remarked as he leaned closer to the table.

"The company is understrength. Most of the rifle platoons have twenty-three, twenty-four, or twenty-five men right now. We only have two officers besides the old man. Two of the platoon sergeants are very young buck sergeants who were PFCs when they got here. Don't get me wrong, they're doing a jam-up job; it's just that we don't have the senior leadership we should have. You're the fourth oldest man in the company right now."

"What's the problem?" I asked. "Replacement system not working right?"

"Oh, the system's working aw'right. Senior NCOs are being slotted for the positions, but as soon as they hit Saigon they start pulling out hip-pocket profiles and pulling every trick in the book to stay out of the bush." He walked over to the big pot and refilled his cup.

"You can go to Saigon right now and find 11-Bravos (Military Occupation Speciality for Infantry) running hotels and recreation centers who ain't spent one friggin' day in the jungle. It's enough to piss the pope off." He shook his head then smiled. "I didn't mean to get on my soap box; let's get back to your situation. You've got thirteen men in your platoon. That's counting you. The platoon sergeant, SSG Dixon, is due to rotate in a month. You don't have a platoon leader right now; brigade's been trying to get us one for over a month. The duds we don't want; the good ones, they don't want to release. It may be a while before you get one. You've got one good fire direction man and two good squad leaders that have been here five or six months. The others have been around for a month or two. One of the mortar tubes had to be scraped, so you've only got two tubes to work with. Other than that, we ain't got many problems," he remarked as he ground his second cigarette out.

★   ★   ★   ★

I learned an awful lot in that ten minutes. I also have to give credit to 1SG Webb for the knowledge I gained during my tour with the "Blue Spaders." He was a first sergeant in every sense of the term. He was liked and respected by all the men of the company. You always knew he would be there when, and if, you needed him. He never stayed back in basecamp when the company was out on an operation; he was with the troops. I remember several occasions when I had to become almost disrespectful to keep him from walking point on search-and-destroy missions.

I'll never forget a somewhat lighter moment that occurred early one morning. We were in an NDP (night defensive position), it was almost dawn, and I was on radio watch. I had just started to heat up some water for coffee when the sound of AK fire broke the silence. Our night ambush patrol had just started back to our position and had been detected by a small VC unit. The patrol leader called in and asked for one of our preplanned concentrations to be fired.

As I was waking up my gun crew, the 1SG, without my noticing him, dove into our pit. While we were busy firing and making adjustments radioed in by the patrol leader, 1SG Webb was busy making a cup of coffee.

About five minutes had gone by and the sporadic small arms fire had stopped, as the VC had broken contact. It was only then that I saw the 1SG sitting on an ammo crate drinking his coffee. He came ready for any and everything—his jungle boots were unlaced; his LBE (load-bearing equipment) was loosely draped over his T-shirt and boxer shorts; his helmet was atop his head; his M16 was in his left hand; and a coffee cup made from a C-ration can was in his right. I laughed and sat down next to him. He slowly turned his head toward me and calmly said, "Damned if I ain't gonna' have to find a quieter place to have my mornin' coffee. Your kitchen's too noisy for me."

★　★　★　★

The company commander, Lieutenant Simms, was a great deal like the 1SG. He was always there when you needed him, and yet he was almost inconspicuous. He demanded a lot from his platoon leaders, especially when we were in the jungle on an operation. In return, the platoon leaders received his full support when needed. If one of the rifle platoons had a buck sergeant acting as platoon leader during an operation, he was the platoon leader. Lieutenant Simms would treat him as such. The views and recommendations of a buck sergeant were given the same consideration as those of a lieutenant. I had always heard that there was no place in a combat zone for a leader that relied on a democratic style of leadership. It was very apparent that Lieutenant Simms had not heard that little bit of wisdom. Naturally, in combat, there are times when decisions must be made instantly by the commander, and Lieutenant Simms handled those situations in a professional manner.

My most common memories of Captain Simms are those of him sitting down, propped against a tree, reading one of his seemingly endless supply of paperback novels, while calmly directing one of his platoons in contact over the radio.

Unlike many of the "Yes Sir" officers, he didn't always agree with directives and orders put out by higher headquarters. He had been in the jungle for over a year, he knew what tactics worked and which ones didn't. He wrongfully gained the reputation at division headquarters of not being a team player. This assumption could not have been further from the truth. We always accomplished our mission, and we managed to do this because the safety of his troops was uppermost in the mind of Captain Simms.

I last saw and talked to Captain Simms on the Officers' Club golf course at Fort Benning, Georgia, in 1970, where he was attending the Infantry Officers Advanced Course. He was riding a golf cart loaded with kegs of beer and, as usual, was taking care of his classmates, making sure they had a good time regardless of the outcome of the golf match. He had put on a little weight and had had a few marriage problems (who hadn't?), but he was still the same guy that had earned my respect and admiration in the jungles of South Vietnam.

★ ★ ★ ★

Sgt. Larry King, better known as "Killer," was my chief FDC (Fire Direction Control) man. He had been with the unit for about six months and knew all the tricks of the trade with the 81mm mortar. He was a little guy, about five foot seven or eight, but he could handle that plotting board in the dark, and faster than anybody I'd ever known. He taught me ways to fire a mortar that couldn't be found in any manual. He was very proud of the fact that the battalion recon platoon always requested fire support from Bravo Company's mortars.

Killer only had one problem during the entire time I knew him. He wore a size five boot and it was next to impossible to find an extra pair. He still had the pair he was issued when he first got to Di An. Our supply system didn't always work the way it should have. He finally traded a cheap pocket radio to an ARVN soldier for a brand new pair. I guess all the small sizes went to our allies.

★ ★ ★ ★

SP4 Don Royal, "the snake charmer," was a big black guy from Mississippi. He was one of the squad leaders who had been with the platoon for about five months. He was strong enough to carry the entire three-piece mortar and most of the time did carry the heavy, awkward base plate.

During his time with the platoon, he had appointed himself the point man during movement through the boonies. In place of the standard M16, he carried a 12-gauge shotgun and a wide variety of shells.

I found out why he liked to walk point and carry the heavier shotgun on my first operation. We had moved about 1,000 meters without incident when Don cut loose with his shotgun. Two quick, loud blasts broke the silence and sent me crashing to the ground.

I knew I'd been had when I saw that no one else had hit the dirt. I quickly got to my feet and rearranged my gear.

"Got that sucker!" the booming voice of Don reached us from his position at the front of the column.

I asked Killer what was going on.

"Snake just reduced the population of snakes in this part of the jungle by one," he replied with his little grin in place.

It was comforting to know I didn't have to worry about being ambushed by snakes as we continued through the jungle.

★ ★ ★ ★

PFC Bob Waters was my RTO (radio-telephone operator). He was a short blond-headed kid from Virginia.

RTOs, as a general rule, should be able to speak clearly and be easily understood over the radio. Bob had two strikes against him right off the bat. He always had a wad of tobacco big enough to choke a horse in his mouth and his Virginian accent required true understanding.

31

It was only natural that he was nicknamed "Cud."

About a month after my arrival, Cud came down with a light case of malaria and stayed in the aid station with chills and fever for about a week.

We were glad to see him when he joined us in the field during Operation Bismark. He had lost a little weight and still made frequent trips to the latrine. After a couple of those trips, we had second thoughts about Cud.

It seemed every time he made one of his trips, we got incoming mortars in the area. I made him give us a warning when he felt a sudden urge so we could grab our helmets and find a bunker. We jokingly thought about changing his nickname to something more appropriate.

★ ★ ★ ★

In the seven months he had been in the platoon, PFC Roy Darrell had become the ace of all trades. He was a draftee from Birmingham, Alabama, and answered to the nickname "Reb."

Reb could handle any job in the platoon, from the guns to the fire direction center, and do each one in an outstanding manner. But he couldn't handle the booze. He had been up and down the promotion ladder so many times in his stay with the platoon that even he was never sure what rank he had at any given time.

"I shore am glad we don't have to sew our rank on these fatigues anymore, Sarge," he remarked to me one day in his slow drawl. "It'd take all my damn drinking money to keep these stripes right!"

Reb left the unit as a sergeant to go back to Birmingham and civilian life. I never saw him drinking, or drunk, when we were in the jungle, and he knew his head had to be clear.

★ ★ ★ ★

SP5 Ray McClintock was the medic assigned to our platoon. Doc, as he was naturally called, was a tall black from Detroit, Michigan. Even though his parent unit ran the dispensary and was based at Phuoc Vinh, Doc stayed with the guys of our platoon when we were back in base camp. He was as much a part of the platoon as any of the other guys.

Doc took his job seriously. He believed in prevention rather than treatment. When he handed out the dreaded malaria pills, he stood there and made sure we swallowed them. He was always harping at us to be sure we took extra socks on an operation.

In addition to his canvas medical bag, which he called his "magic box," he always volunteered to carry some piece of equipment for the platoon. He carried the medics' standard weapon, the .45 calibre pistol, but he always managed to get his hands on an M16 or shotgun when we made contact.

Doc didn't care for the medics that called themselves conscientious objectors. He called them cowards. He told me about one such medic that had been assigned to one of our rifle companies.

"This dude comes boppin' in spreadin' his shit 'round. First thing he lays on the CO is he's a conscientious objector and he don't believe in killing noo-body. He thought they'd send him back to division, see, and he wouldn't have to let everybody see he was just a chicken-shit coward.

"But the ole man didn't buy that shit. He sent him packin' right to the first platoon. They tried to give him a .45, but he wouldn't take it.

"Next day they went out on a road clearing operation

and walked into an ambush. Three or four guys got chewed up pretty bad before they broke contact. When the dust-off came in, this dude shows up with bandages all over his sorry body. He dusted his self off!

"When they got back to the Med-Evac hospital and checked the guys, they ain't 'en scratch on the dude. He just freaked out.

"I don't know what happened to him: We didn't see him again. I hope they hung him by the balls, but I doubt it; he didn't have any."

★　★　★　★

Private Joe Swinney came to the platoon in January 1967 from the hills of Tennessee. He had just finished school and married his high school sweetheart of three years.

Being a true Tennessean, and seeing that the job market wasn't exactly falling at his feet, he volunteered for the army and, after basic training, Vietnam. He had just turned nineteen.

He had been a star running back in high school and quickly became know as "Popeye" because of his strength and build.

We made Joe our platoon mailman because he normally got half the mail anyway. We kidded him that he must be paying everybody in his hometown to write him. If the platoon only had ten letters one day, you could safely bet your last dollar that four of them were for Popeye.

The mail was brought out on a resupply bird one afternoon in late January.

"I'm gonna have a baby!" Joe announced to everybody in the company and any VC that might have been in shouting distance. From that moment on Joe spent every minute of his free time planning the future of his unborn child.

It was late afternoon on the thirty-first of March 1967. I'll never forget that day as long as I live.

We had reached our NDP after walking some six thousand meters. We were west of An Loc at a place called the parrot's beak, near the Cambodian border. Thanks to a few sniper rounds, we had finished digging in our mortars in record time.

The battalion recon platoon was checking the area to our north when they were ambushed by a company-sized NVA unit. We were in contact with the recon platoon leader by radio and had been providing them with protective fires; our fires probably caused the enemy to spring the ambush before they had planned.

They managed to pull back to within eight hundred meters of our perimeter, but not before taking heavy casualties, including the platoon leader, RTO and two other men.

With air and artillery support coming in, volunteers were needed to bring the wounded back to safety. Popeye answered the call one more time.

After successfully bringing one wounded member back to the perimeter, he returned for one more trip. Joe came back later that afternoon; but someone was carrying him. He had caught an AK-47 round in the center of his forehead.

We all cried for Joe that night and for his unborn baby—and his plans.

Chapter 5

WELCOME TO THE NIGHT

I'D BEEN IN THE COMPANY THREE DAYS when our first company-size operation came up. It was a local search-and-destroy mission to be conducted north of our basecamp. Most of the operations during the latter part of 1966 were conducted on a small unit level, the smaller the better. At times, a platoon-size element would be dropped into a location by chopper and left to operate for two or three days alone. They would always be under an artillery umbrella, and another unit, usually from the same battalion, would be designated as a rapid reaction force ready to move on a moment's notice if things got too hot.

All the platoon leaders and platoon sergeants gathered in Lieutenant Simms' small hootch for a briefing. The old man was a firm believer of informal briefings. He sat on his bunk with a rusty can of Carling Black Label in his hand and gave us the details of the operation. We were each given aerial photos of the area we would be operating in. Accurate military topographic maps of South Vietnam were almost nonexistent down at company level. The French army probably left the ones we were using. Aerial photographs were not only easier to get, they were very accurate and the terrain was shown as it actually was two or three days before.

We were going out four thousand meters to set up a perimeter and the line platoons would search the area using a patrol method known as "clover leaf." Simply stated, this meant that three or four units would start from the perimeter going out in different directions for a specified distance, make an arc and return to the perimeter by a different route. A large area could be thoroughly covered using this method, and it was standard operating procedure in the 1st Infantry Division.

A very important lesson learned by infantry units in Vietnam was that of not using the same patrol route over and over again. The VC were both very patient and very observant. If a local guerrilla unit observed a unit using the same route from one point to another more than twice, you could bet your next year's pay that the next time that route was used, the VC would be waiting for you. A small patrol would be ambushed; a larger unit would encounter snipers and numerous booby traps. Unfortunately, with some units, it was only after numerous unnecessary casualties that this simple lesson was learned and put into practice. I was thankful that Lieutenant Simms had already mastered that lesson.

From the very first day of training, the infantryman is threatened to "spread out and keep your distance."

Ideally, a squad of six men should cover about seventy meters in open terrain when on the move. The chances of a grenade or mortar round wiping out a squad could be eliminated if this was done. Human beings are group oriented by nature. Add to that the fear of the unknown, and you have what is commonly called a "gaggle" or "cluster."

The platoon leaders had a saying in the battalion about spreading out and keeping distance. If they saw their formation closing up they would yell, "You guys are gonna get me 'DePuyed' if you don't spread out!''

Maj. Gen. William DePuy, the division commander, had a habit of flying over his units while they were moving to check the dispersion. On one such occasion General DePuy spotted a unit that had bunched up and, getting on the company frequency, called the company commander and told him to get the situation corrected. He flew over the unit again later and the platoon's movement was still bunched up. He had the chopper land and proceeded to find the platoon leader. He told the platoon leader to get on the chopper and left the platoon sergeant in command. When the company commander arrived at the position, he was told to turn the company over to the executive officer because he had been relieved.

Thus the term *DePuyed* was born.

When we left the perimeter of Phuoc Vinh, we had both mortar tubes and fifty rounds of HE (high explosive). When I found we only had thirteen men in the platoon, I had serious doubts about being able to operate two guns with the necessary amount of rounds. My stateside training told me it couldn't be done. Every man in the platoon, even our attached medic, carried either a part of a mortar, or rounds, on their back in addition to their personal gear. We were to be resupplied by air once we reached our position and the perimeter was secure. We might have looked like a band of gypsies when we walked out the gate, but we had everything we needed, and we were ready for action.

Walking four thousand meters through the jungle with seventy pounds on your back in one-hundred degree weather was not an enjoyable walk in the park. Add to that the knowledge that your next step may set off an explosion that could end your life, and you just might be able to imagine how exhausting the trip could be. Even if you were in excellent physical condition, you would be mentally drained. I was in good physical condition when I arrived in Vietnam because I had prepared myself. Although I was only twenty-four years old and weighed the same as I had when I graduated from high school, my time spent on the mortar committee as an instructor hadn't helped my physical conditioning. I started my own PT program in order to get in top physical condition. I exercised and ran two miles every morning and evening for almost one month. I felt sure I was in good shape when I left for Vietnam. I soon learned that having to be on your toes and mentally alert twenty-four hours a day was much more taxing than the physical requirements of combat. The added stress of being responsible for the lives of your men is an awesome burden.

I took the advice of 1SG Webb and added two canteens to my web belt before we left. It's a good thing I did; I sucked the last warm drop from my third canteen just as we finished digging our last mortar pit at our night defensive position. I was a little embarrassed when I had to bum some water that evening to make a cup of coffee.

In my first three weeks with the unit I ate enough salt and drank enough water to be a full-fledged registered Black Angus.

During our movement to the position, I understood what the 1SG had meant when he told me I would like the way the old man operated. Lieutenant Simms literally "walked" the lead platoon all the way to the new position using the mortars. My two guns would leapfrog about every one thousand meters and set up to fire support. We would fire to the flanks and to the front of the lead platoon as it moved. If Charlie was out there, we would be able to turn the table and surprise him and, hopefully, prevent us from walking into an ambush. There is no doubt in my mind that Lieutenant Simms' utilization of the mortars saved many lives. He was a mortar man's dream commander. Some commanders were unsuccessful in their use of mortars because they didn't understand how to use them. They might have had a bad experience with them previously and just didn't trust them. If the mortar platoon leader or platoon sergeant was not proficient or strong in his recommendations, the company commander was deprived of the use of a very important weapon in combat.

It didn't take long for me to learn another lesson. You didn't wear underwear walking through the jungle in this climate. You talk about a rash! This one made jock itch seem like heaven. My pack was a little lighter on the next operation; I didn't carry any underwear.

I remember one time when I wished I did have some underwear on. We were on a search-and-destroy mission just west of An Loc. We had been humpin' almost four hours through some real thick undergrowth in one-hundred-plus degree weather. The jungle was so thick in places we found it necessary to chop and crawl. We all were praying for some rain to cool us off and to cover up all the racket we were making chopping through the bush.

People in Alabama are always talking about the fire ants that seem to take over everything in the summer. They are bad, but they can't hold a candle to the big red monsters that live and hide in the folded-over big jungle palm leaves. Unknown to me, a whole family of these creatures managed to crawl inside the back of my wringing-wet jungle fatigue shirt as I brushed their home. It wasn't very long before they decided to have dinner, and they weren't very particular where they dined! At first I thought hornets had ambushed me. My entire back felt as if it was on fire. Trying to be as quiet as possible under the circumstances, I dropped my gear and tore my shirt off. With a little help from Cud, we managed to scrape the giants off my back.

Just as I was getting ready to put my shirt on, my mind registered another stab of pain; this one came from a very private part of my anatomy!

I dropped my pants and looked down to see one of these red monsters with a death grip on a very sensitive area. He was actually standing with his back legs fully entrenched in my tender skin slapping back at me as I tried my best to knock him off!

When I finally removed him I made sure he would not be able to do an encore. In fact, I took great pleasure in stomping him.

We established our NDP and sent out one ambush patrol for the night. LPs (listening posts) were established around the perimeter and Lieutenant Elbert had our supporting 105s fire in concentrations for quick support in the event we needed them. Radio watch was set up and one last cup of coffee was made before getting some rest. I made sure my three canteens were replenished before I made myself comfortable on the lumpy sandbags of my bunker. I never understood how anybody could go to sleep inside a bunker. I always felt more secure on top of or beside one; at least I could see 'em coming.

I had just finished my cigarette and rolled over when this very clear, distinct sound pierced the black quiet of the jungle. I rolled all the way over on my stomach as I reached for my rifle. Fatigue was no longer a factor; my eyes were wide open as I scanned the dark jungle for any movement. No one else seemed to be disturbed over the sound. Just as I was beginning to think I had imagined the sound, it broke the silence again. I rolled off the bunker and ran in a crouch to one of the gun pits.

"Can't sleep, Sarge?" came the greeting from Killer as I knelt beside him.

"You didn't hear anything?" I asked in disbelief. "I

41

heard the same thing twice just a minute ago. It was just as plain as if you or I said it. Somebody said, 'Fuck you.' Didn't you hear it?"

When I looked around at Killer, I could almost feel the big grin on his face.

"That's a lizard, Sarge. They're all over the jungle. We call 'em 'fuck-you lizards,' " he answered.

I don't recall ever seeing one of the little monsters, but I'm sure I would have had a few choice words of my own for it if I had.

To this day, every time I see a lizard, I always think of Killer and recall that sly grin on his dark face.

Chapter 6

THE CHAINS OF LOYALTY

WITH ONE BIG FIVE-DAY OPERATION UNDER MY PISTOL BELT, I thought I was a seasoned combat veteran. We had not made contact with the VC or seen any indications of recent activity during the entire period. The whole operation seemed like a walk in the park. I couldn't believe everybody was so glad to get back to Phuoc Vinh and start the monotonous routine of maintenance on the mortars. That seemed too much like stateside duty to me. I was ready to take on the entire North Vietnamese Army. Fortunately for me, I soon learned better, and I was glad for every chance to get back to base camp.

I remember one operation when we stayed out for thirty-six days. I was glad to see Phuoc Vinh after that one. My bunk looked better than any Hilton hotel I'd ever seen. We were in War Zone C, providing security for a company of engineers who were rebuilding a bridge. After about two weeks, a chopper dropped us new jungle fatigues and socks. They got there just in the nick of time, because our fatigues were almost to the point of walking on their own. They weren't green anymore; they had turned almost white with all the salt our bodies had given off. It was nice to jump in the river and be able to put clean fatigues and socks on when we got out. The old saying "absence makes the heart grow fonder" held true in Vietnam, too, especially good clean clothes to wear on a regular basis. Things we Americans have always taken for granted became a luxury for the grunts in Vietnam.

Still, lying around the company area at Phuoc Vinh, cleaning, oiling the mortars and conducting crew drill, got old in a hurry. Entertainment back at the base consisted mainly of the nightly showing of old movies. We didn't get to see many of the box-office hits that were playing the theaters back in the States, but that didn't seem to bother anyone. We watched our hero, John Wayne, as he single-handedly won World War II. Surprisingly, the most popular movies we were able to get were of a TV series called "Combat" with Vic Morrow as the star. We jokingly called these our "training films." No night was complete without watching the current episode of Hollywood's version of combat. We at least got a good laugh out of them.

The only other type of entertainment available was the ville of Phuoc Vinh. There must have been at least ten bars in the small village. Most of these were shabbily built tin fronts stuck on to already existing shabbily built homes. The front side contained the bar area; the rear portion housed what was known as the "boom-boom" area. You could get anything you wanted in these hovels; and some things you didn't want, such as strains of VD that still have no known cure. The Vietnamese beer was served over ice (when it was available) and tasted something like what you would think embalming fluid must taste like. The Vietnamese "Ruff-Puffs," what we called the regional forces or local militia, were always around in the bars with their weapons. You would think their sole mission was to protect the "Phuoc Vinh Tea Houses." For some of them it probably was. I'm sure they did a better job of that than going out and fighting the VC. Fights would inevitably break out and, on occasion, rounds would be exchanged. It got so bad at one point that Brigade put out a policy which prohibited arms being carried into the ville by the GIs. Things calmed down for a while after that because you couldn't feel too secure downtown without your M16.

With all this fine entertainment available, it was no wonder that operations into the jungles were sometimes welcomed by the troops. You can only stand so much of a good thing, right? Besides, GIs aren't supposed to be happy unless they have something to complain about.

In late October we became part of an operation known as Shenandoah. Intelligence reports indicated a buildup of a large VC element southeast of Minh Thanh, just north of the Michelin Plantation. Our two sister battalions were to be inserted near the area to check it out. We would be on airstrip alert for an eagle flight—to be inserted on short notice if we were needed. We loaded on the choppers and flew to Lai Khe, east of the big rubber plantation. We sat up just off the airstrip and waited.

Another unit ran into big trouble right off Highway 13 near An Loc. All of a sudden, our plans were changed and we loaded up and headed to Quan Loi.

Quan Loi was nothing more than an airstrip cut out of the middle of the rubber trees. Two or three large French plantation houses tried to add a little class to the remote area but failed miserably. One of the large houses had a swimming pool, which we made use of on later operations into the area.

That night I was introduced to Puff the Magic Dragon, also known as "Spooky." The plane was an old C-47 equipped with miniguns that could fire 6,000 rounds per minute. The plane also carried flares that could light up the entire battle area. There was no other combat sound in Vietnam like that of the minigun when it was fired. All you heard was a continuous growl, the level of the roar dependent on how close you were to the area. Sometimes you couldn't hear it, but you knew Spooky was working out when you looked up and saw an almost steady steam of red tracers falling to the jungle floor. Every fifth round fired was a tracer and at 6,000 rounds per minute it looked like a waterfall of deadly red. As I watched it work, I was glad it was on our side.

After an uneventful night just off the airstrip at Quan Loi, we got on the choppers and headed for Dau Tieng. At least we were getting closer to our original destination. After our arrival, we learned that the artillery unit at Dau Tieng had fired 1,500 rounds during the night in support of our sister battalions just north of us. Both battalions had been in contact with the enemy unit since their insertion in the area. Puff stayed over the area for about an hour before returning to Bien Hoa. Reports monitored on the radio indicated the enemy unit had been surprised in their base camp area and were fighting to escape. Enemy casualities were unknown; ours were described as light.

Air strikes were called in on the base camp. The strikes continued for almost an hour, then the artillery took over. I found it hard to believe that anything could have survived through all that pounding of ordnance.

We prepared for a "hot" insertion as we boarded the choppers once more. We were going in to sweep the area for any stay-behind personnel left by the VC and to give the area a thorough search. Our sister battalions had been lifted out earlier during the air strikes.

The artillery fires were shifted to the north as we made our approach to the LZ. We felt a little better as the lead choppers reported that the LZ was cold. They hadn't taken any fire on the way in or out. We got off the choppers, headed for the nearest woodline, and reorganized quickly.

The VC base camp was located in a dense jungle area

with triple canopy vegetation. A great deal of the ordnance dropped on the base camp didn't make it through the heavy vegetation and went off before hitting the ground. Nevertheless, the devastation caused by the air strikes and pounding from the thousands of artillery rounds only made our trip into the base camp more difficult. Trees were splintered; some still smoked from napalm dropped during the air strikes. The smell of cordite was heavy. I was sure no one could be left alive in this area.

Lieutenant Simms gave us our order of movement and we headed to our destination. The lead platoon, 1st platoon, had been moving no more than five minutes when two quick rifle shots were fired in our direction. The platoon returned the fire and immediately took cover. Lieutenant Simms got on the radio to the 1st Platoon leader and asked what seemed to be the problem. A VC sniper had been left behind to hold up the advance of our unit, thereby giving the remnants of the VC element time needed to escape and disappear. The sniper fired one or two rounds every two or three minutes—just enough to keep our lead platoon occupied. Our artillery FO (forward observer), 2LT Elbert, called artillery in to our front. A FAC flying over our position notified us he could have four "fast movers" on station in about five minutes. Lieutenant Simms requested he get them and let them work out.

The artillery came in so close that we were getting shrapnel from the bursts. About fifty rounds had been fired when Lieutenant Elbert shut them off so the F-4s could drop their load. The firepower demonstration went on for about thirty minutes and then the 1st Platoon moved out again.

About five minutes had gone by when the platoon leader called the CO. They had found a sniper in one of the still standing trees. He was dead. The body count was called in as "KBA" (killed by artillery). The VC sniper really had no chance, or choice. He was a stay behind "volunteer." One of his leaders had tied him to the tree so he wouldn't have second thoughts about his mission.

I recalled a briefing during my in-processing where we were reassured that all available assets of the US military might would be brought to bear on even one enemy soldier when we found ourselves in contact. At that time, I didn't grasp the real meaning of the briefing officer's statement. But after seeing this, I understood. I had just witnessed the whole world being brought down on one lone Viet Cong soldier.

In our search of the base camp area, we uncovered seventy-four dead VC, some left in their fighting positions and others hastily buried in shallow graves. There were blood trails leading out of the base camp in almost every direction. A small number of weapons and ammunition was also recovered.

Chapter 7

RICE AND MORE RICE

IT SEEMED LIKE EVERY HUNDRED METERS we managed to cut through the jungle, we found a VC base camp or tunnel complex, and rice. I had never seen so much rice in all my life. I didn't know there was that much rice in Vietnam.

It was November, and we were on an operation called Attleboro, north of Tay Ninh in War Zone C. We had been operating in the shadow of Nui Ba Den (Black Virgin Mountain) for about two weeks. Nui Ba Den was the highest point in our rather flat terrain area of operation. The U.S. had a signal unit on the top of the mountain. Personnel were resupplied and changed by air. During the rainy season, it was a very rare occasion when the top of the mountain could be seen through the clouds. It was said that the Viet Cong controlled the middle portion of the mountain. Tay Ninh was a large city and its close proximity to the Cambodian border made it an excellent point of entry to South Vietnam for the North Vietnamese coming down the Ho Chi Minh Trail. Due to this the population changed from day to day.

The vegetation was so thick in this area that we found ourselves creeping, literally crawling along the jungle floor. We had to change point men every hundred fifty or two hundred yards so no one would pass out from the heat and exertion of chopping. The sound of machetes hacking through the vines and bamboo made it impossible to hide our location or our intended destination from the enemy. The only people who could have been surprised was our own unit. The VC missed an excellent opportunity to ambush us. We couldn't maintain any type formation that would allow us to spread out and keep a safe distance, because of the thick terrain. At times, if we managed to get three or four feet apart, we couldn't see the man to our front or flanks. At one point, while we were trying to keep dispersed, it took over one hour to move about one hundred meters. In order to maintain contact and insure we reached our NDP before nightfall, we found ourselves bunched up in a single file crashing through the jungle. I know we all felt more secure being able to see each other, but we sure were asking to be wiped out.

We had had very little luck in engaging the enemy in our zone. It seemed they were always one step ahead of us. Signs of recent activity in many of the base camps we discovered during this operation were plentiful. On two or three occasions, smoldering fires and warm rice were found in the kitchen areas.

On one particular occasion, the VC must have been as surprised as we were upon our walking into their safe haven. Our lead platoon had walked through their perimeter of spider-holes and well-concealed fighting positions some fifty or seventy-five meters. The point man walked up to within ten meters of a group of four VC having their lunch. About ten rounds were fired, all M16, resulting in two VC killed and two VC prisoners. They were evacuated back to division headquarters for treatment and interrogation. The results of their interrogation showed they were members of a local VC unit. They were responsible for the procurement of food supplies for two base camps used by larger VC units in the area. The base camps were used by different units as resupply and staging areas. One of the VC volunteered to lead us to a large rice cache not far from where they were captured.

There had been many instances of American units being led into ambush by captured VC who promised to lead them to base camps full of weapons or food supplies. Many times units would waste days and weeks hacking through the jungle following a prisoner who was knowingly leading them on a wild goose chase. This was not such an occasion. Over a period of three days, we were led to four base camps, two of which were connected by an extensive tunnel complex. The tunnel rats, an elite unit of volunteers from the 1st Engineer Battalion, were called in to check and destroy the tunnel complex. These men that eagerly went down into the unknown of those dark tunnels quickly gained my respect and admiration.

The extent of our tunnel exploration was normally throwing a few grenades into the entrance and standing back. If nothing came out before or after the explosions, smoke grenades were thrown in and we tried to spot the smoke escaping from air vents and other openings. If we didn't get any results we would mark the location of the tunnel on our map and move on. The engineers would be notified and the tunnel rats called in.

It takes a special kind of person to crawl down into a dark tunnel with nothing but a pistol and a knife. The rats knew that anything from a battalion of VC to snakes could be waiting for them. Many of the tunnel complexes were multileveled and the main part of the tunnel could be overlooked without extensive searching.

During an operation in early 1967 in the Iron Triangle, we located a tunnel complex that was used as a hospital. Large wards and operating rooms, fully equipped with instruments and lights, were totally underground. There is no way of knowing how many American and ARVN soldiers had walked over that ground before, completely unaware of the activity below.

It also takes a special kind of person to live in those dark, damp complexes for weeks, months, and even years.

In one of the base camps we located what looked to be enough rice to feed half the Vietnamese people. It was piled in a bamboo hootch with a tin roof. The hootch was about twenty feet by forty feet and fifteen feet high. The entire area was covered with rice piled to within four feet of the tin roof. We also found rice in bags with the shaking hands emblem and USAID markings. This was a common finding any time we located a rice cache. In a roundabout way, we were feeding our enemy too.

The jungle was very thick, preventing detection from the air. We established a base nearby and cleared an LZ big enough for two hueys to land in. Then we started moving rice. For two days, there was a constant flow of choppers in and out of the small area. At the end of the second day, we couldn't tell we'd even made a dent in that giant pile of rice. It was decided to make the LZ large enough for a CH 47 chinook to get in and, hopefully, get all the rice out in a little quicker fashion.

The time we spent shuttling rice wasn't all boring and monotonous. The rainy season had gotten underway and every afternoon we got soaked. It normally rained late enough so that our fatigues would not dry out before nightfall. There is nothing more uncomfortable than trying to sleep on hard wet sandbags in wet fatigues—unless you add a few incoming mortar rounds. You tend to forget about your wet clothes for a while. That happened the first night. A couple of guys were wounded, but not seriously. The remainder of the night wasn't very restful.

The second night, the rifle platoons established ambushes at three different locations.

About 0100 hours, the ambush near the large cache of rice reported hearing movement near their site and asked me to fire an illumination round. I replied that due to the thickness of the jungle canopy an illumination round would probably be worthless and suggested that he hang on until he was sure he had movement. I knew who the patrol leader was; he was one of the "shake and bakes" who had been with the company only a month. This was his first ambush, and I knew he was nervous.

No more than three minutes had gone by when the radio came to life again.

"I know I got movement out here by the rice," whispered the patrol leader.

"Give me a coupla' HE and let's see what happens."

Killer and Snake had the rounds on the way in a matter of seconds. The sound of the explosion were amplified by the wet jungle and seemed closer to us than they were.

"Drop two-five and fire for effect!" the patrol leader responded. "I know we got some dinks out here. I heard some screams."

We put five more rounds on the target and got ready to fire in support of the patrol's contact with the VC.

"What's your situation now?" I asked the patrol leader.

"Light the area up. We're gonna' check it out."

About ten minutes had passed when the radio came to life again.

"We got a bodycount, but I don't think they got a category for this kind," said the patrol leader.

"What you got out there?" I asked him.

"We got three monkeys blown away all over this rice! Maybe somebody has a recipe for monkey meat!"

53

★   ★   ★   ★

A lot has been said (mostly critical) about the young "shake and bakes" of the Vietnam era. As in all cases, some of the derogatory comments were deserved and are true to this day, but I don't think these young men received enough credit for accomplishing the job they were called on to do.

They were called a lot of things: shake and bake, instant NCO, boy wonders, and Fort Benning Warriors were the most common. But 90 percent of the time in a firefight, when the chips were down, they were called sarge.

Due to heavy casualties in the lower NCO ranks and a projected shortage of sergeants and staff sergeants, a program was quickly developed by the Infantry School at Fort Benning, Georgia, to put a Band-Aid on the problem.

Young graduates of basic training, both draftees and volunteers, most eighteen- or nineteen-year-old recent graduates of high school, were sent to a six-week cram course. They were force-fed a mixture of "book" tactics and lessons learned from Vietnam, principles of leadership, and responsibilities of an NCO. Upon graduation they were promoted to the rank of sergeant E5 and handed orders for Vietnam at the same time.

These proud young men had, in a mere fourteen weeks, attained the rank that prior to this period men had worked hard for two or three years to reach. It didn't take a genius to know that hard feelings and rejection would be a natural result of this program. They had another strike against them also; they were cheated out of the opportunity to gain one very important thing that cannot be taught—experience.

Now, filled with mixed emotions of eager anticipation and fear, they headed home for a brief stay with their family before continuing their journey to Vietnam. For many it was to be their final visit home.

The huge amount of confidence and responsibility placed on these young men was, to say the least, overwhelming. As a squad leader in an infantry platoon, these green NCOs were given five or six men to lead and take care of. In most circumstances, their squad members had been in Vietnam longer than they themselves had been in the army! They had the experience factor that the squad leader didn't have. The instant NCO knew he had to prove himself to his men; that fact alone is enough to crack most men. Add to that the awesome responsibility a leader has to get his men through a battle alive and in one piece, and maybe you can begin to understand the unenviable position these young men found themselves in.

Although I had no instant NCOs in my platoon, I knew six of these young men very well, as they were in my company. I had many talks with each of them. They constantly asked questions of senior NCOs and took their job very seriously. Four of the six extended their tours in Vietnam, one of whom made the army his career; one was killed in action; the other was wounded and later died from his wounds.

For the ones that survived Vietnam and were reassigned to a unit in the States, they found their problems weren't over yet. For some, the real problems had just begun. Most of them couldn't cope with the spit and shine and dull routines of a noncombat unit. They drank too much, took drugs, got in fights with superiors, went AWOL, and, in general, said to hell with it. A good many volunteered to go back to Vietnam because they felt they could handle Vietnam better than the "Mickey Mouse"

55

of a stateside unit. They were trained for combat and wanted to get back to the only environment they had experience in.

A large number were discharged because they couldn't adjust to military life. They had served their purpose, many heroically, and now the machine that created them didn't want the responsibility of dealing with them.

When the newspapers were full of stories of returning Vietnam vets, high on alcohol or drugs, raping, robbing, killing, and committing suicide, I couldn't force myself to be shocked by their actions. Although I do not condone acts such as those, I can certainly see how they could happen. There were many good "shake and bakes" in Vietnam, but we must take credit for the bad ones, too.

★　★　★　★

We almost had all the rice evacuated and everybody was glad of it. We had been in the same place for about five days, and we didn't feel too comfortable about staying there any longer. Sniper fire had increased in the last day, and we all had a case of the nerves.

A huey slick was hooking up the last sling load of rice to be carried out, and we were going to destroy the remainder with CS and explosives. Just as the chopper had gotten the load about fifteen feet in the air, a sniper opened fire. The chopper pilot, unable to hear the sniper rounds, was slowly gaining altitude. One of the sniper's rounds must have hit the engine and the huey turned on its side and crashed to the ground. The fuel line ruptured on impact and the fuel was spraying into the cockpit of the huey. We managed to get the pilot and co-pilot out of the wreckage before they were seriously burnt by the fuel. One of the door gunners had been pinned in the wreckage when it crashed and had died instantly.

That last load of rice had turned out to be a costly one.

Chapter 8

RELAXATION?

THE SMALL VILLAGE OF PHUOC VINH reminded me of an old Western movie town. The streets and sidewalks were dirt; many of the stores, which were nothing more than clapboard and tin, had packed dirt serving as the floor. You couldn't walk down the sidewalks without stepping on a small kid who was trying to convince you that your boots needed polishing. The homemade shoeshine boxes they carried around were almost as big as they were. Their big brown eyes looking up at you almost made it impossible to turn down their offer, even if you had just polished your jungle boots before coming into town. The older kids didn't want to waste their time shining boots for twenty-five cents; they were more interested in selling you their sister for a "short-time jus' five dolla." Inflation would raise it to ten before long.

The ever present "Ruff-Puffs" sauntering down the sidewalks with holstered pistols swinging halfway down their legs only added to the fantasy movielike set.

The majority of the town consisted of cheap, souvenir-type stores, beer joints, and "Saigon Tea Houses." Black-market American cigarettes and Cokes lined the shelves of every store. On rare occasions you could have your choice of Miller High Life, Falstaff, Hamms, or Carling Black Label beer over the Vietnamese embalming fluid beer in the beer joints.

The Saigon Tea Houses were the busiest places in town. You could get anything you wanted in these establishments, and some things you wouldn't want to take home to your wife or girl friend.

All of these places looked the same. The front contained a makeshift bar with stools and eight or ten tables cramping the small area. American rock and roll, blues, and country music blared nonstop from the already noisy interiors.

The number of girls sitting at the tables or the bar constantly changed, due to the traffic to and from the back portion of the house. The rear of the bar was about twice the size of the front and was divided into eight or ten cubicles, about six feet by ten feet; the only furnishing was that of a makeshift bed about the size of an army cot. When you walked down the hall to one of the cubicles, you couldn't keep from thinking you were in a stable or barn. The size of the cubicles and the sounds and smells that came from them made you think you were walking past stalls filled with horses or cows, all in heat. That is a more fitting description of what was going on in the cubicles than trying to pass it off as "making love."

The smell that was created by the tea houses only added to the already bad smell of Vietnam. When the bar girls had finished their roll in the hay with a GI, they proceeded to "clean" themselves in an already dirty bucket of water in French bidet style. They didn't bother to get the sweat left by a now satisfied GI from their bodies. Maybe you can imagine the odor that clung to their bodies after ten or fifteen trips to the stuffy back rooms in over one hundred degree weather. Believe me, it's one you could never forget!

Oh, yes! I almost forgot one more smell to add to the mixture. A delicacy the bar girls could always find time for no matter how full the house got with thirsty and horny GIs—the eating of a rotten egg! They would boil chicken or duck eggs that were in the final stages of hatching and let them set for a time. Then they would crack the eggs and the feast would begin. If you have ever retched at the smell of an animal that has been dead for some time, you would begin to have an idea of the ungodly smell when those eggs were cracked and the bar girls would eat the whole thing—bones, head, feathers and all; and lick their lips while they told us how good it was! Needless to say, that's one delicacy I have yet to try.

We came back into base camp after five or six days of uneventful road clearing and security missions. We classified these missions as "stateside" or "ho-hum," because we didn't normally get involved in any heavy contact with the enemy, and when we did there was always plenty of help nearby. Even on no-contact operations the mental strain was always present.

I had planned to sleep until the heat forced me out of my bunk. We had cleaned our gear and weapons the evening we got back in, then went over to watch the movie with our mermite can full of beer. After the movie was over and the beer gone, I took a shower to try and cool off before hitting the sheets.

About 0900 hours, Killer and Reb were trying to tear my bunk up.

"Get up! Let's go to the ville and find some action!" Reb was hollering as he yanked my mosquito net down.

"Come on, Sarge," Killer was begging. "Somebody has got to keep Reb out of trouble."

We weren't on standby, and that meant party time for Reb. Killer was right; somebody had to take care of him, or better, protect the village from Reb.

"I got to go see how many times I can fall in love today. Break my record." Reb was pleading now while he tugged at his jungle fatigue pants. It looked like he had stayed up all night drinking in preparation.

"I don't see why you want to pay those slant eyes to get your ashes hauled," I mumbled as I sat up on the edge of my bunk. "You're gonna' wake up one morning and discover a part of your family jewels has dropped off from one of these unheard-of gook diseases."

Reb pulled out a small bottle from his fatigue shirt and shook it in my face. "I got my penicillin, Sarge. Doc takes care of me."

Doc took care of everybody with an endless supply of his "no sweat" pills; but penicillin had little or no effect on some types of venereal disease that flourished in Vietnam.

"Reb, you 'member the last time you went to the ville," Killer butted in, "you said you might as well have taken matters into your own hands and used sandpaper!"

We talked for another three or four minutes, but when Reb had the urge, no amount of talk would change his mind. We went to the ville with Reb and had a beer while he took care of business; then we listened to him complain about that "sorry slant-eyed slope" all the way back to base camp. He didn't hurt her, but he didn't think she should be chewing bubble gum while taking care of him; so he made her swallow it.

★ ★ ★ ★

There were two or three barber shops in the ville that managed to stay busy. They weren't fancy like the ones in Saigon, with their sexy manicurist and stateside equipment—far from it.

The nearest one to the base camp was about one hundred meters outside the gate on the east side of town.

61

It was built with no more than four or five pieces of tin and attached to the side of an old beer joint. There was an entry way cut in the front and one window on each side had been cut from the tin. Some four-by-fours had been nailed together and provided a boardwalk into the barber shop over a ditch that ran between the shop and the street. There was just enough room inside for three chairs for waiting customers and the barber chair, which was sitting on an artillery shell crate.

The barber had to have been in his fifties, but he did the best job he could with the old fashioned pressure clippers and baby powder he used to try and keep sweat off our necks.

Late one afternoon Jackson, our supply sergeant, along with myself and Snake, went down to grab a quick trim before leaving for a seven-day operation. Jackson jumped in the chair first and the old barber went to work. Snake was sitting in the chair that gave him a view out the entrance. I was sitting in the corner next to one of the side windows trying to catch a breeze that wasn't blowing. About five minutes had gone by when Snake jumped from his chair, yelled "Cobra!" and proceeded to knock one side of the tin barber hut down on his way out. Jackson, with shaving cream on his face and still draped with a white cloth, cleared his chair and knocked the other wall down on his way out. With two large exits available I looked out the entry way and there on the boardwalk, gently swaying, was about a four-foot cobra. Without further hesitation, I went out one newly created exit and the barber took the other. The cobra, seeing that everyone had left, turned around and made his way back into the jungle across the street.

It took about five minutes of heavy convincing to get Jackson and Snake back to what was left of the barber shop. We got our haircut, finally, but we never went back for another one late in the afternoon.

★ ★ ★ ★

Mail call was always the highlight of any day in Vietnam, whether in the field or base camp. Even when we were in the jungles on an operation, mail was brought out to us by chopper, if at all possible. I can only remember a couple of incidents where we went for three or four days without mail. It normally came out with the chow or ammo resupply bird. It seemed to make you work a little harder finishing your defensive position before dark, knowing you had some mail from home to sit back and relax with later.

We had our share of the dreaded "Dear John" letters also, from Lieutenant Simms, our company commander, on down the ladder. Some were from wives, most from girl friends. I could tell when one of my men had bad news from home. The hurt showed in their eyes and their faces became creased with anger.

There is never a "good" time for anyone to get a Dear John letter, but it seemed as if the worst time to get one was back in base camp. The sudden unexpected hurt, depression, and anger were only amplified in the relaxed atmosphere of the so-called "rear area."

There were occasions when a Dear John sent an angry, hurt GI, thirteen thousand miles from home, almost to the brink of no return. The depression, mixed with too much alcohol, made it easy to turn against best friends, and, with loaded weapons at hand, attempted suicide was not uncommon.

I was awakened one night by a burst of rifle fire which was very close. I grabbed for my M16 as I rolled off my bunk to the floor of our tent. Even in my half-sleep state, I knew the fire came from an M16 on automatic. It didn't have the heavy sound of the AK-47.

One of the third platoon riflemen had gotten a Dear John at mail call the previous afternoon. He had reached the point where something had to give and had sat up in his bunk and opened fire. He wasn't shooting at anyone, only trying to release his pent up rage. It took what seemed to me an hour to calm him down and take his still-loaded weapon away from him before we could get any sleep. It was actually about ten or fifteen minutes, but time seems to stand still when you are dealing with a hurt soldier with a loaded weapon.

I received a Dear John letter only two months after my arrival in Vietnam. I struggled through a divorce and waged two battles during my remaining months in Vietnam: one against the Viet Cong and the other to win custody of my two-year-old son. I will forever be grateful to a young air force JAG captain at Maxwell Air Force Base in Montgomery, Alabama, and his attorney father, for all the work they did to enable me to gain custody of my son. Some debts can never be repaid.

★　★　★　★

First Sergeant Webb, Staff Sergeant Jackson, and myself had taken Staff Sergeant Dixon to the ville for a couple of beers the day before he left. It was late afternoon, and we were heading back to base camp. The street was almost deserted except for GIs heading back on foot and jeeps full of grunts who had had a little too much "embalming fluid" to walk back on their own.

A skinny dog got a little too close to a jeep he was chasing, and before he could recover, he was lying crushed in the jeep's path.

Before we reached the dog, a distance of no more than fifteen or twenty feet away, five or six small kids had converged on the dead animal and were fighting over who would get it. I couldn't understand why the kids would be fighting over the dead dog. If anything, I thought they would have been upset and mad at the "numba 10 GI" who had killed it.

Top just shook his head and said they were fighting over supper.

The spoils of war.

Chapter 9

ARCLITE

ONE OF THE MOST COMMON OPERATIONS during this time period was called "search and destroy," a very macho-sounding phrase that really didn't fit our actions.

Most of the time when we were searching for Mr. Charles in order to destroy him, we only found signs of recent activity, not the enemy. We did however, manage to destroy many deserted base camps and villages in our searches. Many of these base camps turned out to be a part of a larger tunnel complex that was not detected during our search. The VC were very adept at camouflaging their underground cities. A very good and informative book on this subject was recently published by two journalists who "toured" some of the very complexes we walked over many times while on search-and-destroy missions. The title of the book is *The Tunnels of Cu Chi*.

It was a well-known fact that the VC would not engage an American unit unless they felt confident they could defeat us. They fought only on their terms or when they were surprised in an ambush.

The term *search and destroy* could well have been changed to *stalk and be stalked*.

★ ★ ★ ★

It was the first part of December, and we were in base camp preparing for a search-and-destroy mission that was to begin the next day.

Early the next morning I was brought out of a sound sleep by an ungodly sound. My teeth were actually chattering. I realized after I sat up my whole body was bouncing and my bunk was trembling. Off in the distance there was a constant rumble of what sounded like explosions going off milliseconds apart. The rumbling and tremors went on for about four or five minutes. I knew the sounds weren't coming from anywhere on the base camp. I couldn't understand why I was the only one sitting up wide awake. The other guys that had been in-country awhile only turned over in their bunks and continued sleeping. I didn't know if I should wake everybody and get to a bunker or what.

Killer was snoring in the bunk next to me.

"Killer! What's going on?" I asked as I shook him.

"Arclite," he mumbled.

"Arclite? What's that?"

"B-52s. Go to sleep." He mumbled as he turned over and buried his head under his pillow.

I had just been introduced to the awesome sounds of a B-52 airstrike. Being from Alabama, I was familiar with the freight-train sound of a tornado; I had heard the loud explosions of artillery and the deafening cracks of bombs exploding, but the sound I had just heard was mind-blowing, to say the least. I couldn't imagine what it would be like to be on the receiving end of that payload.

That morning as we were preparing to move out, we learned that our mission had been changed. We were going on a sweep of the area that the B-52s had hit to do a ground BDA (bomb damage assessment). Intelligence reports had indicated that an NVA regiment was using

67

the area as a base camp. As I looked at the map, I realized the area was about fourteen or fifteen klicks (kilometers) north of our base camp. I was going to get to see the destruction of a B-52 strike up close.

During the briefing, Lieutenant Simms told us to prepare for a hot insertion into the LZ. I thought he was being overcautious or kidding. I didn't see how anyone could still be alive after all those tons of HE had been dropped on them, much less be in any condition to fight.

Our company was to be inserted just to the east of the target and sweep through the area to the west. Alpha and Charlie companies would be inserted north of the area and fan out into blocking positions. Two companies from our sister battalion were moving into blocking positions to the south with their APCs.

The magnitude of the destruction was clearly visible from the air as we approached the area. The dense jungle had an area about a mile long and half a mile wide that was no longer jungle. The large, round, bomb craters looked as if they had been placed shoulder-to-shoulder, end-to-end by a giant playing a board game. The entire area was covered by the giant pockmarks. The B-52s had dropped "daisy cutters" to get through the trees and followed them with HE.

We circled our LZ and watched the puffs of dark gray smoke cover the area. The artillery was prepping our LZ in case Charlie was waiting on us. The fires shifted to the east and we went in. We didn't receive any fire and quickly started our sweep.

The view on the ground was quite different from that in the air. From the air you could see a clearly defined pattern made by the bomb craters. On the ground, it was total disarray and destruction. It was an eerie scene, very much like a science fiction movie or a visage of what hell must be like. Huge trees had been uprooted and splintered into toothpicks, and the entire landscape was turned upside down. Remnants of large trees protruded from the ground at odd angles. The sloping walls of the bomb craters were still lined with a thin coating of soot from the explosions. Most of the craters were twenty-five or thirty feet deep and were big enough to bury three or four large trucks in. If at one time there had been a base camp here, it sure didn't exist now.

We had covered about one fourth of the area when Lieutenant Simms started receiving word from the 1st platoon on the right flank of the sweep. Pieces of cooking utensils and various other items were being discovered. Medical supplies were scattered among the debris. An occasional piece of blood-soaked clothing was found draped over a charred log. Then came the reports we had been waiting on. A shattered arm, a piece of a leg, a foot still wearing a batta boot were being discovered.

The search slowed in order to allow more time to thoroughly sweep the area.

We finished the sweep of the entire strike area about an hour before nightfall and sat up our NDP. Alpha and Charlie companies sat up ambushes to the north of our position.

It was difficult to come up with an accurate body count to send to higher headquarters. How would you do it? Take all the arms, legs, feet and other miscellaneous pieces and divide by two? Our first platoon had reported blood trails heading north from the strike area. Later, during a debriefing that included Alpha and Charlie companies, it was reported that thirty-two new shallow graves had been discovered in their area. There was no way of knowing how many more graves were not discovered and how many more were buried later during their escape.

Only God knows how many were buried in the tunnels during the strike.

There was no activity from any of the ambushes that night, and the next morning we were extracted from the area and returned to base camp.

After seeing the total devastation of the area, it was hard to believe that some had escaped and were in good enough shape to drag the wounded with them. I learned later that that was the trademark of the NVA: They took their wounded and dead with them when they broke contact, if at all possible. It was very demoralizing to American units after having been in heavy contact for hours with the enemy to search the area after contact was broken and find no bodies. The Vietnamese used every tactic in the book, and they were good at them all.

★　★　★　★

Pulling security for an artillery fire support base was normally a breather for infantry units. With all those big guns around, it was really easy for a mortar platoon. Compared to the 105s and 155s, our 81s seemed like little pop guns. Even though they made a lot of noise and naturally made no attempt to hide their position, all that firepower gave us boonie rats an extra feeling of security.

The artillery folks, lanyard yankers as we "lovingly" called them, knew how to live in the boonies. When they rolled into a position with all their vehicles and started unloading and setting up, it looked like a band of gypsies had pulled into town! They didn't do without the comforts of base camp—they brought it with them, everything from complete mess halls to steel bunks and mattresses! You could also bet your last MPC that a portable shower point would pop up close by if an artillery unit stayed at a FSB very long.

They always had beer with them and somehow managed to keep it cold. I think half their ammo resupply consisted of ice. On occasion they would share chow with us, but never their beer. If they were in a real good mood and had just been resupplied, they would sell us a few for a buck apiece. That didn't sit too well with most of us, but you would be surprised how much a grunt would pay for something ice cold in the middle of the boonies with the temperature stuck on 110 degrees!

The noise the big guns made constantly being fired both day and night was easy to get used to. I found out very quickly you could sleep through anything if you were tired enough. I slept through rocket and mortar attacks on two or three occasions back in base camp after returning from long operations, without missing a single snore. But one thing I could never get used to around a fire support base was the endless number of supply choppers that were required every day. We were accustomed to the sand and dust stirred up by the slicks that resupplied us. What we weren't prepared for was the debris stirred up by the huge twin rotor chinooks that resupplied the artillery! Everything not nailed down was subject to being blown into oblivion by the strong prop-wash. Most of the fire support bases were located on ground that had been cleared of vegetation. In the dry season, dust was thick enough to eat even when a huey came in; it was unbelievable when a chinook sat down or lifted off. God forbid if you were caught without your shirt on in the open. After it was over, you looked like you had been sand-blasted! Just trying to keep your rifle clean was a full-time job around a fire support base.

During Operation Cedar Falls in January 1967, we found ourselves at a large fire support base in the Iron Triangle. There was one battery of 105s and one battery of self-propelled 155s occupying the FSB. We were sharing the security with an ARVN ranger battalion, the little people who wore the purple berets. They were much better trained than the regular ARVN units and had the reputation of being able to handle their portion of the perimeter.

We had been at the fire support base, nicknamed the "Dust Bowl," about three days. The activity had been light, a few sniper rounds and the line platoons making first light sweeps and some short-range patrols. It was about 2000 hours (8:00 P.M.), and things were pretty quiet for a change. I was lying in Snake's mortar pit, propped up on some ammo crates, smoking a cigarette. Killer had dropped in, and we were discussing what we were going to do when we got back to base camp.

"Why don't we go to Saigon for a day or two?" Killer suggested. "We could always say we were going to check on our other tube."

We still had only two of our three mortar tubes available for operations. The maintenance channels left a lot to be desired in a combat zone.

"Sounds good to me," I replied. "I don't know if my body could handle a nice cool hotel room with clean sheets, though."

"Man, what you mean?" asked Snake. "This body is more than ready for it!"

One AK-47 round directed at the east side of the perimeter, the ARVN rangers' portion, broke the quiet of the night. The rangers returned fire with everything they had, machine guns included, for about one or two minutes. We scrambled for our steel pots and weapons.

The quiet returned after the rangers ceased firing. I had just rolled over on my back, looking up at the stars, when four quick, loud bursts startled me. It wasn't the explosions that made my eyes pop wide open but the four large green tracers that flew over the mortar pit. The ammunition that the VC and NVA used all produced green tracers when fired. I thought all U.S. ammunition produced a red tracer.

"Good God! Did you see that? What did the little bastards run in on us now?" I asked.

"What you talkin' about, Sarge?" asked Snake.

"Didn't you see those big green tracers fly over the pit just now?" I asked, still not believing what I had seen.

"You mean those four rounds just fired?" asked Killer.

"Yeah. I guess." I could sense that little smile of Killer's even before I replied.

"That's just a duster, Sarge. Don't worry, it's ours," Killer replied through his little grin.

I remembered seeing the four tracks with the mounted twin guns pull into the perimeter that afternoon, but I had never seen them in action before. They were really anti-aircraft weapons, but they were very effective against snipers in trees. I thanked the good Lord above that the big green tracers were on our side.

They found the sniper the next morning on a first light sweep, but there wasn't very much left of him.

Operation Cedar Falls was one of the most successful operations for the 1st Infantry Division in January 1967. The big Rome Plows cleared over three square miles of the tunnel-infested jungle in the Iron Triangle. Close to four hundred VC were killed and almost two hundred captured. In addition, almost five hundred threw up their hands and said "Chieu Hoi," which meant they were coming over to the government side under the Open Arms program.

★ ★ ★ ★

73

It was almost Christmas 1966, and rumors were floating around that a cease-fire would soon be observed by both sides. There would be no bombing raids, no artillery (or mortar) H & I fires, and no search-and-destroy operations. In general, it would be a time for peace.

In reality, we were just kidding ourselves, and I think everyone from General Westmoreland on down knew it. The NVA would use this period to freely move down men and supplies over the Ho Chi Minh Trail into South Vietnam. Intelligence statistics showed that tons of material and thousands of NVA soldiers made their way into the battle zone during this time, as in all other times of bombing halts and cease-fires.

Our new battalion commander, LTC Alexander Haig, was taking no chances of allowing the Viet Cong in our area to strengthen their position during the lull. Instead of making booze runs to Saigon or sunbathing on top of our perimeter bunkers, we found ourselves conducting local patrols in an effort to safeguard our base camp and abide by the cease-fire.

LTC Haig, who in a very short time would be promoted ahead of hundreds of his contemporaries to four-star rank and serve a short time as the chief of staff for President Nixon before being appointed secretary of state, lit his shooting star as the commander of the Blue Spaders. He was a brilliant tactician and a polished leader who led by example. He was stern but fair to all, which gained him the respect and admiration of his men, who, out of no disrespect, called him "Big Al."

It was not uncommon on a long march through the jungle to feel a hand on your shoulder and turn to hear LTC Haig asking how you were making it. He didn't make his office in a C & C chopper high above his men, as some battalion commanders did. He preferred to be on the ground, where the action was.

74

On the morning of 1 April 1967, minutes after the end of the biggest battle the Blue Spaders had in Vietnam, LTC Haig was picked up by chopper and carried to a fire-support base, where he assumed command of the division's 2d Brigade and was promoted to the rank of full colonel. The FSB was our direct-support unit during the battle of Ap Gu and was attacked at the same time we were denying us direct support artillery fire. The 2d Brigade commander was wounded during the attack. LTC Haig was picked to take over command of the 2d Brigade, and deservedly so.

Prior to our patrols, we were instructed not to fire unless fired upon, which didn't leave a very secure feeling with any of us. That statement was quickly followed by a reminder that we should take all precautions to protect and defend ourselves.

Although we popped a few caps during this period, we did not become involved in any heavy contact. There were hundreds of cease-fire violations committed by both sides. Most of the casualties we suffered during this time were not due to contact with the enemy but to booby traps and mines. It seems the local VC used the lull to step up manufacturing and emplacement of booby traps in areas they knew we would patrol.

They were, as usual, very effective.

Chapter 10

THE ELEPHANTS ARE COMING!

BOOBY TRAPS WERE ABOUT AS WIDESPREAD AS VD in our AO, and there were about as many types. They ranged from the very primitive homemade punji stakes to more modern explosive devices, such as the claymore.

The punji stake traps were made from bamboo and were used in many different ways. In the early stages of the war, the most common of these was a foot trap. They were small square or rectangular holes in the ground with razor sharp bamboo stakes stuck in the bottom and sides of the hole. The stakes would easily penetrate the thick soles of the jungle boot. The nylon/cloth upper portion of the boot likewise afforded no protection from the sharp spikes. To make the traps more effective, the sharp points were often dipped in feces to create infection. These traps ranged in size from the small foot trap to large deep holes able to accommodate the entire body.

Punji stakes were also used by the VC in their ambush positions. Ditches or low areas covered with vegetation in and near the kill zone would be filled with the stakes and camouflaged. They knew we would hit the ground in those areas when they popped the ambush.

It was only after American units had occupied or conducted numerous operations in an area that the more modern booby traps began to appear. Even though these booby traps were more effective and deadly, they were still primitive because most were homemade.

Hundreds of names would not appear on "the Wall" today if we had only been more careful about the trash we left in an area when an operation was ended and we split. Americans are litterbugs by nature, and we were no different 13,000 miles away from home. The VC became scavengers and turned our waste into deadly weapons that came back to haunt us.

The thousands upon thousands of empty C-ration cans left along a route of march or at an NDP were policed up by the VC and made into booby traps; the miles and miles of WD-1 commo wire left at a position due to a hasty departure or out of total neglect gave the VC a means to detonate a booby trap or mine from a safe distance. Live ammunition, including grenades, claymores, belted machine gun rounds, and small arms rounds left in a fighting position vacated because of enemy pressure, or because a tired grunt was trying to lighten his load, only added to the ever-growing enemy arsenal.

Larger items such as dud bombs and artillery and mortar rounds that were policed up by the VC were either rigged for command detonation or busted up to get the powder in order to manufacture many more explosives.

In a very real sense, we were supplying our enemy for months with ammunition to kill us with. It took long enough to sink in, but the lesson was finally learned. Before we left an area, all our trash was buried, even cigarette packs and paper. If we stopped to eat while on the move, our trash was buried in individual holes before we moved on. We took a page out of Charlie's book and booby trapped our large trash dumps around areas such as fire support bases and large NDPs before we left. We might not have stopped the scavenging completely, but now they were having to pay a price for our garbage.

There is no possible way to explain the frustration felt by a unit that has been confronted by booby traps day after day. Returning from routine patrols with four or five casualties after no contact and not even seeing the enemy tends to get on your nerves very rapidly. The pressures build up, nerves become raw and on edge, and tempers get short. Before you realize it, you are ready to fire up anything or anybody that crosses your path.

I remember a period of about two weeks when we suffered this frustration. In the end the unit wasn't the only one to suffer. I'm sure some innocent Vietnamese suffered too. We had been set up next to a small village for about six hours while one of the platoons was on a cloverleaf patrol of the area. We had noticed the villagers were not as friendly as most we had patrolled near. Just as we were saddling up to move to a new position, a loud explosion came from the area where our 2d Platoon was preparing to move out. Within five seconds the whole company opened fire in the direction of the village. It took ten or fifteen seconds to stop the barrage when we finally realized what caused the explosion. There was no return fire coming from the village, and there never had been.

It seems a new man in 2d Platoon was getting up from a prone position when the word to move out came. A branch or a vine snagged on the pin of a hand grenade hanging loosely from an ammo pouch and went off. The new man was killed instantly and the members of his platoon, thinking a VC claymore had been detonated, or a booby trap set off, immediately opened fire.

I don't think any of the villagers were seriously wounded or killed, but they sure weren't any friendlier when we finally left the area.

I don't approve of destroying villages or killing innocent civilians, but I fully understand how these instances could happen under such circumstances. Guerrilla warfare, where the enemy is so elusive, only tends to complicate matters. The innocent looking man and woman working in a rice paddy during the day could very well be (and many times were) planting booby traps at night to blow you away. There comes a point when the pent-up anger and frustration must be released. You could only hope and pray there were no innocents in the way.

★ ★ ★ ★

A special forces camp near Tay Ninh requested ground support from the division in November. They had been getting reports from their operatives and civilians in Tay Ninh that they were going to be attacked within one or two weeks. Although the camp was small and pretty much isolated, the A team had done an excellent job of establishing its defenses.

We set up on the edge of a rubber plantation, after making sure we could safely fire our mortars over the trees in order to get max range, and began digging the mortars in.

We had been in the boonies for about two weeks on Operation Attleboro when we got the word to move to the SF campsite. We were part of a large task force including the 25th Infantry Division, the 196th Light Infantry Brigade, the 173rd Airborne Brigade, and at least two ARVN battalions, hoping to find and destroy the elusive COSVN HQ.

It was a known fact that the NVA had been using Tay Ninh City as a mixing point after coming across the Cambodian border into South Vietnam. This was a major factor in locating the SF camp in the area.

We had been resupplied and had just finished settling the baseplates of our mortars when 1SG Webb came over.

"Let's go over to the camp and have a talk with the operations sergeant, Puckett. Maybe he can fill us in on what's goin' on." He sat down on a stack of ammo crates and lit up a yellowed C-ration Pall Mall.

"I may know somebody in the detachment good enough to talk 'em out of a beer or two," he grinned. "Besides, I ain't never been inside a big bad Green Beanie camp before. Might learn somethin' 'bout gorilla warfare." The grin widened as his eyebrows raised about an inch.

I told Killer where I was going as I got my steel pot and M16.

"Get with battalion and check on the patrols for tonight and get the DEFCONs plotted. We'll fire 'em in when I get back if they want us to," I said as we headed for the camp.

The camp wasn't very big, no more than seventy-five yards in diameter, but its defenses were very formidable. Triple rows of concertina wire dotted with booby traps and every possible type of early warning device encircled the camp. It could have been hazardous to your health just walking through the main gate.

A large moat filled with punji stakes was behind the first row of concertina wire and surrounded the camp. The fighting positions around the berm of the perimeter were complete with overhead cover and reinforced with concrete. There were four mortar pits inside the camp, all lined with concrete. The team house was located in the center of the camp and connected to the commo bunker by a tunnel.

The activity inside the camp was quiet as individual cook fires were being readied near bunkers and sleeping quarters. Most of the fighting positions and machine-gun bunkers were not manned. In fact, there couldn't have been more than thirty or forty strike-force members in the camp.

Top was having the same thoughts I was.

"God, if this is all the people they have, I can see why they hollered for help. I'd hate to know this was all I had to operate with. Half of 'em are probably VC."

"Surely they have more than this in their force. Maybe they have a patrol still out," I offered.

"Jerry Webb! You little bastard!"

We turned in the direction the loud voice came from. Standing in the entrance of the team house, dressed in tiger-striped pants and OD T-shirt, was the source of the voice. He stood about six-foot-four and must have weighed two-twenty-five.

"I can sleep good tonight. The U.S. Army has sent Jerry Webb to watch over me!" The big master sergeant's face gleamed as he stuck out his hand.

"Puckett," Top started seriously. "I know why we're here now. This big ugly pollock is afraid of his own shadow. He even has to have a light on so he can sleep. How in hell are ya', Tom?" Top asked as he shook hands.

After a short introduction, MSG Bronski gave us a grand tour of the camp. We found out the camp was understrength. Between combat losses, death threats from the VC, and deserters, the camp strength was about one hundred.

We were in the commo bunker enjoying a real cold Budweiser (in a bottle! not a rusty can) while Sergeant Bronski was filling us in.

"What's goin' on that ya'll can't handle, Tommy?" asked Top.

"Well, a lot of funny things have been happenin' around here lately. One day a lot of new people come into

81

Tay Ninh with all their belongings. The next day a lot of people move out carrying everything they own with 'em. This has been going on for about two weeks now. It's not the same people just moving around. Most of the ones leaving have lived in and around here all their lives. They have to know something's cookin' to just pull up and leave home lock, stock, and barrel." He got up for three more beers.

"Our little people working for us in Tay Ninh say the local VC are making arrangements for a new, major unit to move into this area. The folks at Group think it might be an advance element of COSVN moving in. I'm not so sure that's it."

"What kind of activity, contactwise, you been having in your area lately?" asked Top.

"That's the funny part," replied Sergeant Bronski. "No increase in activity or contact with the dinks in about two weeks. If COSVN was moving in here, you can bet your sweet ass the activity is going to increase. Things are just too quiet."

Top lit another cigarette and asked, "If things are so quiet, why all the reinforcements?"

It was then that we heard the kicker. Sergeant Bronski lit a cigar and slowly exhaled the smoke.

"Two of our most trusted and reliable agents in Tay Ninh were killed two days ago just hours after giving us this latest information."

We followed him over to the big operations map hanging on one wall of the bunker. He pointed out a spot on the map not far from where we were and continued.

"A new NVA regiment is going to cross the border here, and take over this area where we are." He looked at Top and grinned as he continued. "This outfit has brand new equipment, which includes elephants. My people called them the Elephant Brigade. Laugh if you want to, but can you imagine what a herd of elephants could do to a place like this?"

We weren't laughing yet, but we were having difficulty keeping a straight face as we looked at Sergeant Bronski.

It seems some isolated outposts along the border had reported sighting enemy units using elephants to transport equipment, and the intelligence people were beginning to think a new NVA unit would cross the border at this point.

It was getting late as we thanked Sergeant Bronski for the hospitality and headed back to our position. Outside the gate, Top looked at me and said, "They should have sent a mechanized unit in here instead of us. I don't think M16s would bother elephants much. I never did like elephants, not even circus ones." We were still laughing when we walked into our company position.

That night, the platoon had a good laugh too, when I told them why we were there.

It's a good thing we didn't hear any distant rolling thunder that night; we might have all had heart attacks!

We stayed in the area for about four days running local patrols and sweeps during the day and ambush patrols at night. Just as Sergeant Bronski had said, not much was going on. Other units of the large task force were reporting contact with Mr. Charles almost constantly. The war was still raging everywhere except in our little corner of the world.

Even during this lull in the action, bad luck continued to plague us. Not our company directly, but a sister company of the battalion.

The company mortars were firing in DEFCONs for an ambush patrol late one evening. For some reason, the squad leader in charge of the ambush set up in the wrong location. It could have been an honest mistake in reading his map, or he could have gone to the wrong location on purpose; maybe he didn't want to walk the full distance to his designated patrol site and set up when he found what he thought would be a nice safe spot to spend the night. This happened on occasion and became known as "shamming on ambush patrol."

Whatever his reason, the outcome was very costly. The mortar platoon knew where the patrol was supposed to be located and had the position plotted on their FDC plotting board. The first round they fired landed in the middle of the patrol. They were using only one tube to adjust the fire and only one round was fired. The patrol leader evidently had made one more mistake in judgment and kept everyone together instead of spreading out. One soldier was killed and three wounded. The patrol leader was the one killed.

Combat is a stern teacher. The results are absolute and final.

★   ★   ★   ★

The only excitement in my platoon during this period happened to me early one morning.

I developed rather quickly an intense fear of sleeping inside a bunker, any bunker, in base camp or even in the boonies. I had visions of being inside a bunker when we took incoming mortars or rockets and being buried alive as the result of a direct hit. I thought it was kinda' like digging your own grave. I decided to take my chances in the open where I had room to move.

I had gone to sleep on top of the FDC bunker. It was hot and I had used my poncho liner for a pillow. The hard lumpy sandbags didn't provide a very comfortable bed, but there weren't very many comforts in the boonies anyway.

I woke up just as the sun began breaking through the leaves of the rubber trees and, as usual, reached for my morning wake-up cigarette. I raised the top part of my body and propped myself up on my side with my elbow. Just as I was lighting my cigarette, I heard Cud stirring around behind me on the ground. I was fixing to lie back down to enjoy my cigarette when Cud said, "Don't lie back down there! Roll over the other way, quick!"

Not knowing what was going on, I did just as I was told. I rolled over and off the bunker.

There, in the crack of two sandbags, where the base of my neck met my poncho liner, rested a nice-sized scorpion. He had found a nice cozy, warm bed for the night. Now, he seemed to be a little disgruntled that he had been disturbed and assumed a defensive posture. A cold shiver ran down my back as Cud crushed him with his steel pot.

I quickly developed another habit: that of checking sandbags before I sacked out.

Chapter 11

NIGHT MARCH

IF YOU HAVE EVER GONE FOR A NICE PEACEFUL WALK in the woods or a National Forest, I'm sure you have experienced the calm serenity and still quiet of Mother Nature. At times you feel the silence has become deafening when only your footsteps are heard. The forests in Germany are such places. They are well manicured and kept spotless. The German people have long used these stately sites for long relaxing walks and meditation.

I remember a long walk we took through a rubber plantation at night. It was the exact opposite of everything I mentioned above.

Our mission, in military terminology, was to seal a village. In everyday speaking, we were to move about twenty-five hundred meters, under the cover of darkness, through a thick, abandoned rubber plantation, completely encircle a village, and get into positions that would block anyone trying to escape from the village the next morning when an ARVN battalion moved in to search the village for suspected VC. All of this was to be accomplished by a group of approximately two-hundred-fifty grunts (my battalion) and quietly.

Sounds simple, right? Wrong!

We had been on similar missions with the ARVNs before when they had either screwed things up royally or had not even shown up at first light. We sealed a village once before and found we had wasted our time. The ARVN battalion showed up at the wrong village!

We had been on the move all day and couldn't really get fired up for such a dangerous trek. We hoped the rubber plantation was, in fact, abandoned. It could have been the base camp of the unit we were searching for. The latest intelligence reports indicated the plantation had not been worked for months, and no enemy activity had been reported since that time.

The weather forecast for the night didn't help matters, either. There would be no rain to cover the sounds of our movement through the thick plantation, and the moon would be producing all kinds of light because it was due to be full.

As it turned out, the moonlight was not a real hindrance. The thick canopy of the rubber trees didn't allow one moonbeam the chance to hit the ground. The darkness inside the plantation was unbelievable. I had been in dark places before and many since, but none to match that night. It was so dark you couldn't hold your own hand in front of your eyes and make even the shape out. If I had a nickel for every whispered cuss word uttered that night, I'd be on vacation in Honolulu right now. I probably voiced enough to pay for the airline ticket myself.

To make matters worse, somebody in the battalion had had a brainstorm on how we could maintain contact with each other during the march. Right before dark, we all got in a long line in the order of march. The lead man in the column had commo wire tied to the back of his pack. Each man behind him was connected to the commo wire on some part of their equipment at four- or five-foot intervals. So here we were, Alpha Company, Bravo Company, and Charlie Company, tethered to each other like a herd of elephants, fixing to cover twenty-five hundred meters through a rubber plantation in the dark! We all made bets on how long the line would remain connected.

It didn't take long after we started moving. The two-hundred-yard bet was the winner. The line was broken and abandoned before our lead man in the column entered the plantation. I found out why about twenty-five yards into the woodline. A ravine about twelve feet deep crossed our path. I can imagine what it must have felt like to suddenly find yourself being yanked down the slope and becoming a part of a human landslide! It was a miracle that Alpha Company didn't have some serious injuries before better judgment took over and the commo wire link was cut. We ultimately had to rely on shouted whispers being passed down the line to warn us of upcoming obstacles. Our efforts to be quiet lacked conviction.

After numerous collisions with the radio on Cud's back, I grabbed a strap of the radio harness and managed to keep upright for the remainder of the trip. Behind me, Reb had a death grip on my pistol belt and was constantly stepping on the heel of my boots.

The motion of the long column was much like that of a yo-yo during the entire trip. When the lead element hit a clear area and sped up, we had to hang on for dear life; when they slowed down or stopped, we stopped abruptly. We must have stopped twenty or thirty times during the march to check our location and catch our breath. Those brief stops constituted the only times we managed to be quiet. It is almost an impossible task to be quiet moving mortars during the day when you can see where you are stepping. In the pitch black dark of night, it is impossible. Every clang of the tube hitting a rubber tree echoed through the plantation. Naturally, the clang was followed by a muted curse and numerous loud whispers of "Hold the friggin' noise down!"

Early in the morning we reached the point where Charlie Company broke contact with our element so they could move into their blocking position. Realizing that he was the last man in the column now that no one from Charlie Company was holding on to his gear, our trail man from 3rd Platoon was forced to become more attentive to sounds from his rear. About five or ten minutes had gone by when word was passed up the line that we had movement to our rear. The column was stopped and we reoriented ourselves to the rear, awaiting further word.

The next word (or partial word) we got was "It's Charlie!" Not waiting for further instructions, weapons were clicked off "safe," and we prepared for the worst.

When we got the "real" word from the rear of the column, it was "It's Charlie Company coming back." We all let out a large sigh of relief.

Charlie Company had miscalculated and had left our line of march at the wrong location. Keeping an accurate count of your pace and the distance traveled the way we were traveling was not very easy. The pace man had to be a good mathematician to keep up with our two steps forward and one step backward method of travel! About ten minutes after we started moving again, Charlie Company found their correct point of departure and went on their way. Thankfully, we didn't have any further movement to our rear.

We reached our blocking position about 0300 that morning. It was still pitch black and very difficult to get in a good position and even more difficult to set the mortars up. We did the best we could and waited for a little light to make final adjustments.

To make the whole night a complete success, as soon as I sat down to grab a few winks, it started raining! It felt nice, but we sure could have used it hours before to put a damper on all the noise we made plowing through the rubber trees. I didn't get much sleep, but at least I was cool.

When we were roused at first light, we were surprised to find that we were all linked up and the seal was complete. The ARVN battalion showed up at the right time and right village and began the search. The people in the village, who were known to be VC sympathizers, were surprised, and a large number without proper identification were detained. Ten or twelve were killed in the village or while making an attempt to escape.

The mission had been a success, but it sure could have been a disaster.

★   ★   ★   ★

After an uneventful night we were air-lifted out of the area the next morning to another location in the Iron Triangle. An ARVN battalion had walked into a large base camp and tunnel complex and had taken heavy casualties. We were to be inserted about 1500 meters from the base camp location where the ARVN battalion had established a defensive position. While the unit was reporting sporadic sniper fire, they were not engaged in heavy contact at the time. We naturally planned for the worst and prepared for a hot insertion. The lift company of slicks that was going to insert us must have been briefed that the battalion was still engaged.

Vietnam served as a testing and proving ground for the helicopter. The use of the helicopter in its many roles was more than effective and praised by all the professionals and experts in the field. As a med-evac vehicle, the dust-off chopper saved countless lives. A grunt wounded in a firefight could be back in a large field hospital in a matter of minutes, bettering his chances for survival. These dedicated pilots picked up the wounded in darkness or daylight, in most instances in the middle of heavy fighting, without regard for their own personal safety. I remember one pilot who set his chopper down at night in a spot he would have had second thoughts about in the light of day. If we were willing to mark our location, they were willing to come in. If there were any real heroes in Vietnam, the dust-off pilots would stand head and shoulders above the rest of us who served. They will forever hold my respect and admiration.

The cobra pilots, the spotter pilots, and the slick pilots who flew supplies and were our taxi to the combat areas were no less than exceptional in their accomplishments. I have no intentions of slighting the many valorous missions these young pilots participated in. Only one instance marred the many hours I spent in a helicopter. And it happened on this mission.

One company had already been inserted and was on the ground moving to their rally position when my chopper made its approach to the LZ. No reports of choppers taking fire had been received, and it was evident by the movement of the company on the ground that no fire was being received. There were only five of us on the chopper: Snake, his gun crew, myself, and my RTO, Cud.

With the chopper bouncing and vibrating from the down-wash of the rotor blades, the pilot hovered the craft about ten or fifteen feet from the ground. I was sitting in the door ready to get off when the door gunner tapped my steel pot and motioned for us to jump. Not understanding, I turned to him and yelled, "What?!" Again, he motioned for us to get out. Quickly checking the LZ for any signs of incoming fire and not seeing any, I turned toward the pilot and mouthed, "Why? What's the problem?"

The aircraft commander frantically began motioning for us to get off the chopper.

Here I am with four men, each carrying between sev-

91

enty-five and eighty pounds on their back and a complete mortar, and these guys are telling me to jump ten or fifteen feet to the ground.

The longer I hesitated, the more altitude the chopper gained. I had no choice but to take a chance. We quickly threw the mortar out the door and jumped. No sooner had my feet hit the ground and I rolled to my back than I saw our chopper had sat down on the LZ. Showing no understanding whatsoever, I raised my M16 up and aimed straight at the pilot. He immediately threw up his hands and shrugged his shoulders, then begged for understanding with hands pressed together beneath his chin. Snake convinced me I shouldn't fire by knocking my M16 to the ground.

I still don't know what really caused that fiasco to take place. I have convinced myself it was due to the age of the chopper and possibly the power loss and no blame should be placed on the pilot. I was only concerned about being able to function once on the ground, and the safety of my men. Luckily, with the exception of a few black-and-blue bruises, no bones were broken and the mortar was undamaged.

We tied in with the ARVN battalion and established our defensive position. Prior to nightfall, we got a resupply of mortar rounds and we felt a little more secure. Ambush patrols were established and reported to battalion headquarters. Artillery DEFCONs were planned and fired in as our company ambush patrols adjusted our mortar preplans. In anticipation of enemy activity during the night, we went on 50 percent alert. That meant if there were two men in a fighting position, one was awake and on watch at all times.

About 2100 hours (9:00 P.M.), an LP 100 meters out from our 1st Platoon reported he had movement to his front. He was instructed to let the situation develop. The next word we got from the LP was that an estimated ten VC were moving in his direction, and he and his partner were pulling back to the perimeter.

I was just about to drop an illumination round down the tube when all hell broke loose. The sounds of M16s, M79s, M60 machine guns and hand grenades filled the air. At first, most of the fire was outgoing, but it didn't take long for the return fire to start.

There was one strange thing about the sounds of the incoming fire—it all sounded the same. No sharp crack of an AK-47 or SKS, and the incoming tracers were red, not green.

I dropped the illumination round down the tube and told Cud to get on the radio to the old man.

Just as the illumination round lit up the area, screams of "Cease fire!" began to echo along the perimeter, and the firing quickly died down. We suddenly realized an unnecessary and unfortunate accident had just happened.

One of our sister units had sent an ambush patrol out and the patrol had unknowingly walked into our position.

Whether the other unit had neglected to report the ambush patrol to higher headquarters (as was required) or higher headquarters had been negligent in keeping tabs on unit locations was not known. Someone had made a mistake, and a very costly one. Of the eight men in the ambush patrol, four were wounded and one killed. We were lucky; we had no casualties.

I don't think anyone got any sleep the rest of the night even though we were on 50 percent alert. When you have had a bad experience like that, it's hard to forget in a short time period.

Chapter 12

PALACE GUARD

COMPARED TO PHUOC VINH, Lai Khe looked like a resort area. It was about twelve miles southwest of Phuoc Vinh and a little closer to Saigon. The biggest portion of the camp was nestled in a rubber plantation, which added to the lush tropical look. Even though the trees had been thinned out, the shade did wonders to cool the tropical hootches. They almost reminded you what air conditioning felt like. The flagpole was the biggest shade producer we had in our area at Phuoc Vinh!

Lai Khe served as the base camp of the division's 3rd Brigade headquarters and three infantry battalions: 2d/2d Infantry, 1st/16th Infantry, and 2d/28th Infantry.

The looks of a plush resort area was as far as it went in comparing Lai Khe to other base camp sites. While Phuoc Vinh was known as the division's "outpost," Lai Khe became known as "Rocket City." There were tunnel complexes all around Lai Khe and the VC seemed to use the big base camp as a training target. It was very unusual if a single day passed without the camp receiving at least one incoming rocket or mortar round. All those rubber trees did look nice, and they were cool, but they also caused more damage from incoming rounds because airbursts allowed the shrapnel to cover a larger area. Workers were constantly plugging holes in the tin-roofed tropical hootches.

During Operation Cedar Falls, my battalion was assigned to Palace Guard at Lai Khe. Palace guard was a term we used instead of plain old perimeter guard for a large headquarters element. One or two of the infantry units based at Lai Khe were out on an operation, and someone had to be brought in to secure the perimeter. We had been walking around the Iron Triangle behind Rome Plows for about a week, providing security for the engineers. At least one of our units made contact every day. The VC didn't seem to appreciate our wrecking their base camp areas and tunnel complexes. The Iron Triangle had been one of their strongholds for many years.

We welcomed the chance for a break in the action. We didn't get to sleep in the hootches, but it was nice just being next to them. We did get somewhat of a break in that we were able to use existing fighting positions instead of digging new ones. We did, however, dig our mortars in. I had become a firm believer in adding a covered section to our pits for ammunition storage and equipment. They took a little longer to complete, but when the rounds started zipping in, it sure was nice to know you didn't have to leave the safety of the pit to get a resupply of mortar rounds.

Work never stopped on our gun pits. As soon as the pits were deep enough and the gun had been fired in, work began on the ammo addition. When that was finished, we began to connect the pits by a trench line. Time permitting, trench lines would be completed, connecting the FDC bunker and other personnel areas. Within two or three days each position in the platoon could be reached without exposing ourselves to enemy fire. The many hours of extra work proved to be invaluable on many occasions. Our mortar positions became a trademark in the battalion.

About this same time, the entire division adopted a

new fighting position that got a lot of publicity, both good and bad. It became known as the "De Puy" or "1st Division Fighting Position." Diagrams and directions for the construction of the positions were printed and distributed to non-divisional units with a strong recommendation that they be utilized.

Up to this time, the most commonly used infantry fighting position had been an open two-man position with a dirt or sandbag berm encircling the hole. These positions normally had no overhead cover to protect the grunts from rocket or mortar fragments. They did provide one thing the De Puy position did not allow for: the grunt's ability to view a full 360-degree area to his front, sides, and rear. That is the only complaint I ever heard voiced about the fighting position. Old habits are hard to break, and the grunts wanted to be able to see what was coming at them, and I sure didn't blame them for that. Once they understood the rationale of the position and experienced that first fire fight inside one, they couldn't understand how they had survived without them as long as they had.

The position basically was the same as the old position, only with overhead cover, a thick, built-up berm covering the entire front, and a firing port located at each corner. Entry to the fighting position was gained from the rear. The thick front portion of the bunker consisted of dirt, sandbags, logs, or a combination of the three to make that part as thick as possible with the available material. The idea was to make it strong enough to withstand the impact of an RPG or mortar round. The overhead cover was made of logs or limbs and layers of sandbags.

You might ask, "How in the world do I defend the front of my position when I can't even see to the front?" just as the grunts did at first.

This factor is what made the fighting position so

unique and effective. With the small firing ports located on the sides of the position, fires from one position were directed across the front of the next position. When a company or battalion set up in a defensive posture utilizing the new fighting positions, mutual support and overlapping fires were attained. Maximum protection was provided due to the small firing ports, instead of the whole front being open, and the overhead cover for protection from incoming mortars.

There is no doubt in my mind that the De Puy Fighting Position saved many lives after being employed. The extra time required for construction of the position was minor compared to the added security it provided. My whole battalion can attest to that after an experience on the 1st day of April 1967, at a place called Ap Gu.

★　★　★　★

Our first day and night at Lai Khe was one of those ho-hum periods. We only had a total of ten incoming rockets: five that afternoon and five later on in the night. The normal artillery and mortar counter-fires were shot, but no one seemed to get real upset because after all, the rockets were expected, and no one was wounded.

One of the rifle platoon leaders rejoined the unit the next morning. He had been on R & R to Bangkok and had been back just long enough to pick up his gear in Phuoc Vinh and get to Lai Khe. He and Lieutenant DeVane, our current platoon leader, were the best of buddies. Lieutenant DeVane had an R & R coming up, and he was planning on going to Bangkok, too. Naturally, Lieutenant Vincent came over to our platoon area to fill Lieutenant DeVane in on all the hot spots to check out when he got there. He entertained us with war stories of a different type for about two hours. When he left to go back to his platoon's area, we were all hyped up and ready to go to Bangkok.

The remainder of the day was spent routinely, as we were supporting the rifle platoons, who had squad-size patrols out on local sweeps of the area.

We took advantage of the larger PX at Lai Khe and stocked up on cigarettes and other items not always available at Phuoc Vinh, like books and magazines, snacks and packets of Kool-Aid.

The water we occasionally had to get out of streams and bomb craters didn't leave a very good taste in our mouth. The water purification tablets we added didn't help very much. We tried to keep a supply of Kool-Aid on hand to camouflage the taste of the water. It made a world of difference. Most of the guys had mentioned in letters home how we used Kool-Aid and packages from home were normally loaded with every flavor made. There was always that long stint in the boonies of three weeks or more when everybody exhausted their supply, so we were always on the lookout for Kool-Aid.

A few of my men went over to a 4.2" mortar position located about three hundred meters behind our pits and struck up a conversation. It seems all the four-deuce platoons at Lai Khe had gone in together and built their own club. They had just finished putting the final touches on and had it stocked with beer and snacks. Before the guys returned to our position, they had wrangled an invite for all of us to attend the "Grand Opening."

That evening I split the gun crews, and we went to the club in shifts. Three or four of the guys didn't drink, and I wasn't worried about not being able to function in case we were needed. I went over with the first bunch around 1800 hours (6:00 P.M.). We didn't think the four-deuce people would want an officer in their club so Lieutenant DeVane had borrowed one of Doc's shirts and was going with the second crew.

The club was a smaller version of the tropical hootch with a counter built in at one end that served as the bar. The furnishings consisted of five or six tables made from ammo crates and ten or twelve chairs of mixed and unknown origin. The tape player sitting behind the bar was playing country music and trying to compete with fifteen or twenty loud voices. The four-deuce guys looked and sounded like they had been there all afternoon "getting ready." Four or five guys from an artillery unit had been invited also. The beer was a dollar, but we didn't mind it: These guys had worked hard on the club and spent their money to stock it.

It didn't take Reb long to sucker some of the other guys into a beer-guzzling contest. He'd been dry for over a week, so he had plenty of room. Our hosts mistakenly took his slow way of talking, along with that down-home Alabama drawl, as a sign that he was already four sheets in the wind and wouldn't be able to handle it. He won about twenty dollars and all the beer he could drink before he ran out of takers.

We left about 1930 (7:30 P.M.) so there would be some beer left for the second crew when they came over. That is, we all left except Reb. He was doing some serious beer drinking and a little arm wrestling on the side. I figured he wouldn't get into any trouble with Lieutenant DeVane there, so we left him there.

It was about 2200 (10:00 P.M.) when the second crew came crashing and stumbling through the rubber trees back to our position.

Reb was between Lieutenant DeVane and Snake; I wasn't sure who was holding up whom. Doc's shirt was hanging on the lieutenant's body by a thread, and Snake had blood on his shirt. There was a cut over Reb's eye and a dribble of blood from his nose.

"What in hell happened?" I asked Lieutenant DeVane.

"We showed 'em! We wrecked the place. The whole damn place!" Winston, one of the assistant gunners was mumbling behind them as he tried to catch up.

"What happened?" I asked again.

"There was a little misunderstanding," Snake growled.

"Reb got a little carried away," replied Lieutenant DeVane. "We had to regroup and pull back."

"Not 'fore we showed 'em! Ain't that right, Reb?" Winston slapped Reb on the back, and they both almost tumbled over.

There was a devilish grin on Reb's battered face as he began to explain. "One of them damned lanyard yankers called me a grunt, and we started to have at it, and the LT jumped in 'tween us. Everything was cool 'til he opened his mouth again. He looked right at me and said 'Alabama and Bear Bryant ain't shit!.' Can you believe that bastard said that?"

I asked Lieutenant DeVane, after everybody had settled down, how much damage was done to the club. He assured me the club was still standing and only a few tables and chairs had been demolished. He also assured me we, and especially Reb, were no longer welcome to the club.

I thought everybody in the USA knew you didn't badmouth Alabama and Bear Bryant, even in Vietnam.

★ ★ ★ ★

A somber-looking Lieutenant Vincent paid us a visit bright and early the next morning. The look of satisfaction his face had displayed yesterday and the tone of his voice had changed to those of embarrassment. After a brief conversation, Lieutenant DeVane brought him over to my location.

It seems Lieutenant Vincent had brought back a little surprise from Bangkok. The sweet little thing he had spent four days and nights with had lavished him with more than love and left him with more than just a few moments of bliss to remember her by.

Knowing the army frowned on lieutenants who conducted themselves in a manner other than gentlemanly and above reproach, even in combat, Lieutenant Vincent was between a rock and a hard place. Talk of new division policy which threatened disciplinary action against any officer with a venereal disease only made his problem worse.

After a great deal of moaning and groaning, Lieutenant DeVane came up with a solution. Since no one in the aid station at Lai Khe knew Lieutenant Vincent and would not recognize him, or for that matter any of us, the situation was easily taken care of; we would simply change his name and rank for a short time.

Lieutenant Vincent took his shirt off and as quick as a flash became a PFC by the name of Darrell. Reb was still a little out of it and became the unanimous choice for a visit to the aid station by proxy.

A very young, highly embarrassed lieutenant left for the aid station looking very much like a young, highly embarrassed private.

The old saying, "rank has its privileges," didn't apply when it came to VD.

By the time we left Lai Khe, Reb had left his mark on numerous places of the camp—one he wasn't even aware of.

101

Chapter 13

A RIDE IN THE WOODS

HAVE YOU EVER LEFT HOME FOR WORK ONE MORNING and suddenly realized you should have stayed in bed? I'm sure you have, just as we all have at one time or another.

I got that feeling one morning as we neared a small village. A vile smell permeated the area. It was one we had smelled before. We had been moving for about two hours, and the sun had already made itself felt. The closer we got to the village, the stronger the odor got. The villagers of this particular village were known VC sympathizers and had been for many years. Our first thoughts were maybe an ARVN battalion had come through and destroyed the village and all its people, but that wasn't the case.

The ARVN had another way of handling villagers that aided the VC, and they brought their message home clearly. When the bodies of dead VC could be identified and connected with a family or a village, the ARVN unit would take the bodies to that village and lay them out, as if on display, in the center of the village. It was a crude but effective way to let the villagers know their actions were no longer a secret. That is what happened in this small village and was the cause of the smell.

There were four bodies placed on the side of the trail at the entrance to the village. Inside the village, four or five huts had a body laid out in front of the doorways. In the center of the village, neatly arranged in a row, were ten additional bodies. Two or three of the bodies had been covered with cloth by families.

What few villagers we saw as we moved through the village showed no visible grief. The only plain visible emotions were the stares of hatred that followed us through the village.

I said this book was not going to involve politics, pro or con, but the role played by politics and politicians was so all-consuming that I feel I have to renege on my word, at least temporarily.

I wondered at times, and I still do, if we weren't going in the wrong direction in trying to attain our psychological goals. The politicians kept saying we must win over the hearts and minds of the Vietnamese people. If we could do that, we would surely win the war, because in actuality that was the war. The people would turn to the government for protection and support and the VC would eventually lose the will to fight. Sounds reasonable, right?

Then, however, we turn right around and drop in on a village of 3500 people, mostly farmers, move them off their land and out of their homes with only a few personal possessions to a "resettlement" village on the outskirts of Saigon, and then with fire and explosives, completely wipe their village off the map. Sure, we temporarily hurt the VC in the area, but at the same time, we gained an awful lot of enemies and lost another round in our psychological war.

This happened on 8 January 1967, at a village called Ben Suc on the western edge of the Iron Triangle. Numerous other small villages suffered the same fate during the war, which virtually turned Saigon into a huge refugee camp. Was this the right way, the American way, to win the hearts and minds of the Vietnamese people?

It can be said that many, if not most of these villagers

103

were either VC or VC sympathizers, but I still have my doubts as to the final results.

★ ★ ★ ★

When we started out that morning, we were on our way to a location north of Tay Ninh in War Zone C where a battalion of the 196th Light Infantry Brigade had run into a world of trouble. They had walked into an ambush and had suffered heavy casualties. One of our sister battalions had gone in to relieve them and had suffered casualties, also. All of this had taken place only a couple of days ago.

A division LRRP (Long Range Reconnaissance Patrol) team had been in the area since that time and had reported continuous movement of large troop elements all around the area.

It was late afternoon when we reached the site the 196th unit had been extracted from. Our movement had been slowed by sniper fire the entire day. The area was dense with vegetation, and we cautiously resorted to using a well-traveled trail through the jungle to speed up our progress. Not a very wise thing to do, but we were lucky this time.

Right on the edge of the clearing, in the middle of the trail, sat the last thing I would have ever guessed would be found in these surroundings. Smashed and riddled with bullets sat a jeep with the markings of the 196th Light Infantry Brigade. I never expected to see even an APC in terrain this thick, much less a jeep. I couldn't keep from questioning the feasibility of taking a jeep along on an operation in this part of the country.

The use of the word *clearing* in this instance is a little misleading. The entire extraction site consisted of the trail and a hastily cleared out portion of no more than ten yards on each side of the trail for about twenty yards along the trail. The PZ was so small and dotted with the trunks of chopped-down trees that it would have been very dangerous to even try to land a slick in the area. The chopper would have had to sit straight down and lift straight up in order to get out. I don't think there were very many hueys in Vietnam at this time that had enough power left to even attempt something like that. The unit must have been extracted by chinook using rope ladders. The big chinooks always drew a lot of fire from the enemy, but it would have taken forever using the smaller huey.

Daylight was almost gone as Lieutenant Simms got the company's NDP established. We used the small clearing as the command post and began the task of trying to get the mortars dug in. We only had one place to set them up: right in the middle of the trail, and I'll never forget how hard that ground was! We were only able to dig down about two feet. By filling sandbags with the dirt we had managed to get up, we were able to stack about three rows of sandbags around the shallow pit. The ground was so hard I was afraid the base plates would slide out when we tried to settle them so we could fire accurately. We finally got them settled, but we had to waste about six rounds to do it. With no time for resupply, I sure didn't want to run low on rounds in this particular part of South Vietnam.

Our perimeter that night was somewhat small because the jungle was so thick. The line positions were no more than fifteen to twenty meters out from the command post. No ambush patrols were sent out. We all circled the wagons that night. Having everyone in so close might have made us feel better, but it wasn't a practice to make a habit of.

105

The position seemed to exude an eerie feeling on its own. Knowing what had happened here only hours before strengthened the feeling. The fact that we only had sixteen rounds of HE, one illumination and one WP (white phosphorous) increased the pucker factor considerably. I had one of those feelings that there wouldn't be much sleep this night, and there wasn't. I kept two men to man each gun and sent the rest to fill in positions on the perimeter. I didn't like to do that, but the guys were used to it by now and didn't really mind. The company was so understrength that everybody chipped in more than their share. My mortar guys had almost been on as many ambush patrols as had the line platoon grunts.

It started about an hour after the sun went down. The line platoons were reporting movement all around the perimeter. The radio was very busy. Lieutenant Simms notified battalion we had activity but no contact as of yet. Battalion notified us that the LRRP team, located four or five thousand meters forward of our position, had recently reported a company-size element moving in our direction. Lieutenant Simms calmly alerted the platoon leaders of the report. In a voice void of excitement and filled with confidence, he instructed them to be alert and to hold all fire unless they were sure they had a target to engage. The platoon leaders had authority to pop a claymore if they thought it was necessary before opening fire. Defensive artillery fires would be on the way shortly and would be available all night if needed. Lieutenant Elbert, our artillery FO, was on the radio to our support unit calling for fires at that time.

The VC had recently added a new trick to their already full bag of goodies. Before they began a probe of our perimeter, they would locate the position of our claymores. At that point, if they were sure they had not been detected, they would very carefully pick the claymore up, turn it around, aim it back at our position, and stick it back in the ground. After they had repositioned as many as they safely felt they could, they would move away from the back-blast area and make enough noise to hopefully cause the unsuspecting grunt to fire his claymore.

Unfortunately, until the word got around, it worked more times than it failed. If the GI was trying to see the results of his handiwork when the claymore went off, his chances of being killed or wounded were very good. Those 600 little steel balls didn't have eyes; they could care less which way they went or who they hit when they were fired.

On more than one occasion it had also backfired on the VC while he had the claymore in his hands. At that distance it didn't make any difference which way it was pointed. The results were one gook scattered all over the perimeter!

In an attempt to try and stay one step ahead of Mr. Charles, we used a small piece of reflecting tape attached to the right rear of the claymore. If the tape could not be seen by the grunt who placed the claymore in position, he knew without a doubt that somebody was messing with it and could take proper precautions if he did have to fire it. Using the tape eased a lot of nighttime nerves.

Some units went one step further and booby trapped the claymore with a hand grenade when they set it up. This was very effective too, until Charlie grew to expect the hand grenade.

The night had a special way of playing tricks on your vision, especially if you were tired from walking all day beating the bush. Even if you were wide awake and not the least bit groggy, the bushes and trees started moving. Not really, but in your mind, they did. If you concentrate on one object long enough, all of a sudden you're willing to bet your last dollar that it's moving. The army teaches new recruits to use a scanning, overlap method of observing during darkness. This method is meant to keep your head and eyes moving back and forth over the area you are observing, so any change of position of an object will be easier to spot. It sounds practical and easy, and is, when you are back at Fort Benning knowing nobody is going to shoot at you. In the jungles of Vietnam, all practical things seem to get misplaced. When someone has reported movement, the only thing practical a young grunt is thinking about is survival. That bush he thinks has been moving toward him is in grave danger of being fired up, without any questions first.

The artillery started coming in about one hundred meters out from the perimeter. Lieutenant Elbert marched it all around the perimeter, bringing it in closer and shifting it out. Those big booms sure were reassuring to us.

"We're blowing a claymore." Lieutenant Simms' radio came to life. The message from the 2d platoon leader was followed shortly by the smaller explosion. Fire from M16s were right behind the blast. At least two positions thought they saw something and opened up. The old man told Lieutenant Elbert to get illumination over the area. Two more claymores were fired in rapid succession, followed by M16 fire.

"We've got two dinks KIA for sure," the second platoon leader reported. "My man's fixing to throw a grenade."

A smaller explosion immediately filled the air. This one was followed by a short, loud scream and a few very choice curse words.

One thing you don't do in a densely vegetated area: throw a hand grenade!

The grenade had bounced straight back and landed to the rear of the two-man position. Both of the guys were exposed when the grenade detonated.

When they were brought back in to our location, I think they were more embarrassed than hurt. Both had shrapnel all over the backside of their bodies, and some of it was in a very uncomfortable place.

Lieutenant Elbert cut the artillery off so the dust-off could get over the area for the pick up. Both of the men were picked up by the dust-off, using a sling.

We breathed a sigh of relief when the dust-off left the area and had drawn no enemy fire.

The artillery fires were started again and Lieutenant Elbert kept them going for the rest of the night.

About an hour later, sounds of a heavy fire fight north of us could be heard in the distance. Maybe that company of VC had walked into an ambush in their haste to avoid us.

The two guys that met us back in Phuoc Vinh with their rear ends wrapped in white gauze felt a little better when we told them we had found three very dead VC in front of their position that morning when the area was checked.

Chapter 14

AP GU

LIKE SO MANY SMALL TOWNS OF RURAL AMERICA, Ap Gu was so tiny and insignificant the topographers didn't even bother to list it on the maps. The small village was located west of An Loc near the Cambodian border at a place that had been nicknamed the "Parrot's Beak."

In only two days, the Blue Spaders brought an end to the years of anonymity the small village no doubt had enjoyed. Regrettably, those two days proved to be a lifetime for some while only seeming like forever to those of us who survived.

The engagements of Vietnam were unlike those of Korea or World War II, where clear lines were established and the contested ground went to the victor of the engagement. In those conflicts, fighting over a certain piece of real estate would go on for days and weeks before being decided.

The total madness of a typical firefight lasted only minutes in Vietnam. If an engagement was still going on after ten minutes, it was thought to have been a "major" contact. The battle of Ap Gu lasted hours on both days. It was by all standards a major battle. It was the most significant battle the Blue Spaders had in their five years of combat in Vietnam.

Even with the passage of almost twenty years, the events that took place in those few bleak hours seem to

110

have happened only days ago. If I live to be 100, I feel certain that the memory will still be fresh in my mind.

The battle took place during Operation Junction City, the division's largest operation up to that time. The operation lasted approximately fifty days, through the middle of April 1967. By rotating a few members of each platoon at a time, I think we managed to get everyone back into Phuoc Vinh for clean clothes and a well-deserved day or two of rest during the operation. This was one time Phuoc Vinh looked real good and the chance to get back in was more than welcome.

Near the end of March, the battalion made an air assault into an area near the small village of Ap Gu. Intelligence reports indicated the presence of base camps and fortified positions in the area, and they were right. For two days, in any direction we turned, we found base camps of varying sizes, all with fortified fighting positions. These were not rest areas or supply points, but fortified base camps for a large unit.

There had been three major contacts in as many weeks in the AO since Operation Junction City began. Documents captured as a result of these contacts identified regimental elements of the 9th VC Division. We didn't know it at the time, but three regiments of the well-trained division had suffered heavy casualties against American units since Junction City began. The one remaining regiment, the 271st, was at that very minute "rehearsing" for their all-out assault on our battalion. The regiment's strength was estimated to be around 2500. Our battalion field strength at that time was close to 375, which was about normal. A few of the company regulars were not in the field at this time for various reasons. Captain Simms, who had recently been promoted, was on a long-overdue and well-deserved R & R. Lieutenant DeVane, our platoon leader for the past couple of months, was no longer in the

111

company. Once again, I found myself in the shoes of the platoon leader. A captain, assigned to battalion head-quarters, assumed command of the company while Captain Simms was gone.

Captain Wilson was a tall, young, blond-headed officer I had known while at Fort Benning. He was cut from the same mold as Captain Simms. He had worked with the company once before and knew most of the men and our capabilities. We couldn't have asked for a more competent replacement. He eventually assumed command of the company when Captain Simms went back to the world.

While discovering numerous fortified base camps, contact had been very light, almost nonexistent. We found the usual number of booby traps and experienced a few occasional pesty sniper rounds. We were fixing to put a "ho-hum" classification on the operation until the afternoon of 31 March. Mr. Charles put a damper on our optimism.

We had covered an awful lot of ground that morning before arriving at our destination. We established our battalion perimeter in a cluster of trees that formed somewhat of a circle. The center of the perimeter was fairly open and void of trees. A large clearing, about three hundred meters wide by eight hundred meters long, lay next to our perimeter on the west side. This clearing was a pre-planned LZ called George.

We began digging in our positions about 1200 hours (noon). My company was to occupy the western portion of the perimeter next to the LZ. We tied in with Charlie Company to the north and Alpha Company to our south. Charlie Company's portion of the perimeter on the east and northeast was next to the woodline, not open as was our portion next to the LZ and Alpha's to the south.

Thankfully, the texture of the ground was sandy, and we had easy digging and had managed to get both gun pits about three feet deep in less than an hour before hitting the more compacted dirt beneath the surface. Having reached a normally accepted depth in such a short period of time, the guys were content and started filling sandbags to go around the pits. Work shifted to digging the FDC bunker and gathering timber for the overhead cover.

I was sitting down with the radio talking to Lieutenant Johnson, the battalion reconnaissance platoon leader. He was preparing to leave on a reconnaissance patrol of the area to our north and northwest and was requesting that we provide him close-in fire support on his route out and return to the perimeter.

Just as I gave the handset back to Cud, I heard a voice from behind telling me the positions were not deep enough. Just a little red under the collar, I quickly turned to see who was trying to tell me how to run my platoon and discovered I was alone. No one was there. I shrugged my shoulders and started to blame it on the sun, when I heard the voice again. "You should make those positions the best you have ever built. Go a little deeper and put extra sandbags on top."

I'm sure you have had thoughts, or ideas, come to mind: We all have, at one time or another. This wasn't a thought, or a visual idea. It was a small voice, one that I'll never forget.

I debated with myself for a short time before conceding to the advice of my mysterious mentor. It turned out to be the most important decision I had ever made in my life, and more importantly, in the lives of my men.

For very understandable reasons, however, my men were not overjoyed with their new instructions. A helping

113

hand, from somebody upstairs who knew I could stand a little persuasive power occurred, as if on cue, in the form of two sniper rounds only inches above our heads. Renewed digging began instantly without further complaints.

We had just finished adding another foot to the depth of Snake's gun position and resetting the mortar when Cud told me the recon platoon was north of our position, preparing to check the woodline across the clearing at the northern edge of the LZ. Lieutenant Johnson wanted us to "walk" him into the area by shifting rounds to his front as he entered the area.

We had fired about six or eight rounds to the patrol's front and right flank when the distinct popping sounds of AK-47s interrupted the quiet. The loud crash of grenades or claymores joined the increasing volume of the AK-47s.

It seemed like forever, but was actually only seconds, before we heard the platoon's M16s and M79 grenade launchers return the fire. I was on the radio trying to get Lieutenant Johnson to see where he needed fire, but I couldn't get an answer. I knew he would be trying to get his platoon organized into a defensive posture and laying down a strong base of fire, and I knew he didn't need me bothering him. I dropped the radio and yelled for Snake to start pumping the rounds out on the last fired position.

When a mortar is firing at close range, at a distance of no more than one thousand meters, the high arc of the round makes you wonder if it's ever going to hit the ground. Snake had about five rounds in the air before the first one hit the ground. A total of ten rounds hit in the target area in rapid succession. The ripples of the last explosion had not died after rolling across the open LZ before a deafening cascade of fire was launched by the VC. Heavy machine gun fire, RPGs, and rockets could be heard clearly, mixed with the small arms fire.

The radio's squelch popped and came to life. The sounds of the firefight could be heard in the background as a voice shouted, "Add two five and fire for effect! Don't stop! Keep 'em comin'!"

The soldier gasped for air while the radio was still keyed and began pleading for help.

"Six and six romeo (Lieutenant Johnson and his RTO) are dead. We've got wounded. Please get us some help! It must be a whole company of the little bastards. We need some help. Please."

Lieutenant Elbert had the heavy guns on the way. A bird dog was circling lazily overhead preparing to guide in the air support that battalion had requested. Charlie Company was called on to get to the trapped platoon and rescue them. I had to release some of my men to occupy the now vacant positions on the perimeter. We were still in radio contact with a recon platoon member, who was bringing our mortar rounds in closer to their position. I tried to keep him as calm as possible by telling him about all the help on the way and that things would be all right.

When he marked his position for the bird dog, we could see the yellow smoke drift above the trees no more than twenty-five meters inside the woodline.

"Tell him to put his load just to the north and west of my smoke and he can't keep from hittin' 'em. Don't worry about getting too close to us. We ain't got no choice!" With that last remark, the radio became silent.

The artillery fire was cut off when the F-4s arrived on station ready to go to work. The FAC, in his slow-moving bird dog, had been fired on when he marked the target for the four jets, but he had managed to avoid any damage while regaining a safe altitude to observe and direct the fighters.

We knew we were in for a fight when the jets came

115

in for their first strafing run and drew heavy machine gun fire from the VC. Instead of hunkering down in search of protection, the rate of fire actually increased. The heavy volume of fire directed at the jets indicated not only that they were well dug in in fortified positions, but also that the unit was a large force, or it would not be equipped with heavy machine guns.

We watched as Charlie Company, under the cover of the diving jets, slowly approached the trapped platoon's position. One of their elements, literally crawling in the open of the LZ, began receiving attention from the VC, which all but halted their progress. Mortar and RPG explosions were bursting on our side of the woodline on the northern part of the LZ.

The four F-4s, having dropped all their ordnance, returned to their base to refuel and rearm. We tried to take up the slack with artillery and our mortars while we waited for the next group of fast movers to arrive.

The firing was still heavy, and the recon platoon was quickly approaching the point of running out of ammunition. Word came down that volunteers were needed to bring back the wounded.

I looked at the seven men I had remaining back on the guns and repeated the message. Before anyone else had a chance to speak, Popeye and Winston grabbed their weapons and steel pots, and made their way to the perimeter where the rescue party was forming.

With the new jets making their bombing-run approaches, the rescue members left the relative safety of the perimeter and dashed into the LZ. They eventually reached a position just short of the woodline, where the wounded had managed to gather. The trip back was both dangerous and slow due to the condition of the wounded.

The jets on station at that point—I lost count of the

number of sorties we had that day—must have had some heavier ordnance on board, because the firing had died down. Maybe the VC were running short of ammunition too.

Although not a complete stoppage, the lull afforded the opportunity for the 2d Brigade's 1st Battalion, 16th Infantry to be air-assaulted into LZ George as much-needed reinforcements. The battalion immediately took up positions on the west side of the LZ.

During the insertion, the rescue members got the first group of wounded back to our perimeter. When I looked around for Popeye and Winston, Doc told me they had gone back for more wounded.

With the help of the 1st/16th on the west, Charlie Company had reached and was able to secure the position of the remnants of the recon platoon. Cobra gunships were working the area underneath the F-4s. At one point, I looked up in the air and was amazed at the number of aircraft in such a small space. It's a miracle that none were shot down.

It was about two hours after the fight had started that Charlie Company and the rescue members made it back to our perimeter. Doc had a makeshift aid station set up next to Sergeant West's gun position, doing what he could before the wounded were moved to the battalion aid station.

Exhausted, sweaty GIs were lying and sitting all around our position. Their faces were masked with blank expressions. I spotted Winston propped against a gun position and walked over to ask him if he and Popeye were okay. Just as he looked up and started to answer me, I heard Doc yell.

"Damn it, no! Popeye!"

I couldn't see the body beneath Doc until I moved his

convulsing shoulders to the side. Joe had made one trip too many. He had been hit in the center of the forehead and surely had died instantly. I covered his face and we carried him to the battalion aid station. I couldn't stand to see that face without the ever-present smile.

There may be a macho saying or old belief that grown men don't cry, but I'm sure it doesn't apply to combat. I cried. And I cried for a long time after I said good-bye to Popeye at the aid station.

They said we had killed over eighty of the enemy that afternoon, but there was no joy in the big body count. Our casualties were pretty high, too: seven killed and thirty-eight wounded.

Even though our casualties were high, it could have been much worse. By walking the recon platoon out with our mortars, we caused the VC to prematurely spring their ambush before the platoon had reached the maximum killing zone.

At least I felt good about that.

The enemy had finally broken contact and withdrew to the north. The artillery and F-4s shifted to the north with them. Cobra gunships continued to fly over our area as the dust-offs came in for the wounded, and resupply slicks brought us more ammunition. We had fired all of our mortar rounds at the beginning of the contact, about fifty, and had borrowed some from Alpha and Charlie Companies. We had about seventy-five rounds after being resupplied, hopefully more than enough to get us through the night.

Without a word of prompting, work quietly resumed on the gun positions and FDC bunker. By nightfall, we had the best positions I had ever seen.

About an hour before dark, we got something we all needed badly: a big morale-booster. It came in the form of hot food, brought in by chopper from our mess hall back in Phuoc Vinh. To top it off, they were A-rations, not warmed-up C-rations. No doubt LTC Haig had a little something to do with that decision.

Staff Sergeant Riley, our mess sergeant, brought an extra mermite can of hot coffee out. He knew it would hit the spot with me and Top. It didn't last long, either. Guys who never drank coffee before sucked it up that night. There would not be much time for sleep, anyway.

No ambushes were sent out that night, only LPs established by each company about fifty meters in front of the perimeter. Everybody else manned the perimeter. We had one or two "Spookies" in the area for a couple of hours in case we needed them. The artillery fired a stepped-up version of H & Is most of the night. It was well after midnight when we decided to try and get a little rest.

Everything was quiet—much too quiet.

★   ★   ★   ★

It was sometime between 0400 and 0500 (A.M.). I was asleep on top of the FDC bunker when I heard a voice. I didn't know if I was having a dream, or my mysterious mentor was talking to me again. I rolled over, rubbed my eyes and looked around. Killer was standing beside the bunker, hovering near my face.

"Killer!" I screamed in a loud whisper. "You almost scared me to death! What the hell you want?"

"Let me have a cigarette. I can't sleep," he answered.

I sat up on the edge of the bunker, and we both had a cigarette. Killer was sitting on the ground with his feet hanging over and into the entrance to the bunker. I lay back on the bunker, wide awake now, using my steel helmet for a pillow, looking up into the night sky. It was

still very dark, and there was not a star to be seen anywhere. I remember making a comment to Killer as he went
back into the bunker that it looked like it might rain.

I had just closed my eyes when I heard the distinct
"thunk" of a mortar being fired from a distance. Killer's
head popped back out of the bunker's entrance.

"Is that what I think it is?" he asked. I grabbed my
M16 and steel pot, and we both started yelling as loud as
we could.

"Incoming! Incoming! Get in a bunker, hurry!" The
shouts were being echoed all around the battalion position when the first rounds hit right outside our perimeter.

I took advantage of the very few seconds they required
to adjust the rounds onto our positions to make sure all
my men were in a covered position.

They were fast. Just as I reached the entrance to the
FDC bunker, the next volley was impacting inside our
perimeter. Dirt was showering down on us from the logs
and sandbags on top of the bunker. The rounds kept coming in; I began to wonder if they would ever stop.

Under normal circumstances when the VC were har-
assing us, we could expect five or ten rounds at the most.
No one had to tell us they were going to hit us as soon
as they cut the mortars off.

We were poised and ready to make a dash for the gun
pits as soon as the incoming slacked up. Instead, the
tempo increased. Some of the explosions didn't sound
like mortar rounds, but it wasn't until after the battle was
over that we learned the VC were using 75mm pack howit-
zers along with the mortars.

I got on the radio to find out where our artillery support was. That's when the picture got much darker. In a
coordinated effort, the VC had hit our fire support base
at the same time we were hit. Our direct support artillery

unit was engaged in a fight for their own lives.

It was at that point I knew we had to get our guns in operation quick, or it would all be over.

I could tell by the "crumping" sound of the rounds that they had moved away from our location and were impacting on the northeast portion of the perimeter, in Charlie Company's sector. I told Killer and Cud we had to get out of the bunker and get the guns returning fire before the VC hit us with their ground assault. As they were grabbing their steel pots and weapons, I had another talk, the first of three that morning, with God. I remember very clearly saying, "Please help us, God, and we'll do the best we can."

We left the bunker and dashed for the nearest gun pit.

It was no more than ten yards between the FDC bunker and Sergeant West's gun pit, but I learned an awful lot in the short time it took to cover that distance. Number one, there were more than mortar rounds landing in the perimeter. The holes that were appearing in the sandbags as we dove in the pit were meant for our bodies. The sniper fire could clearly be heard outside the bunker between mortar bursts. Number two, the heavy cloud cover could possibly keep the jets from providing us with close air support. And last, but not least, a sniper had shot out the lights mounted on our aiming stakes! We could do without the aiming stake lights, but I knew we couldn't make it without air and artillery support.

I got Snake's attention in the next pit and managed to get the message across that we had to get some rounds on the way, quick. I told him to start at a range of two thousand meters, aiming directly north, and bring them in toward the perimeter at fifty-meter intervals. Sergeant West would start at a range of 1000 meters and walk them in. I was sure we would hit something within that range; if not the mortars, maybe the advancing VC assault forces.

We managed to get around inside the pits by bending over or crawling on our hands and knees, without too much concern of getting hit. Both guns were firing within a few seconds.

The majority of the incoming rounds were still impacting in Charlie Company's sector. An occasional stray landed in our area, but not enough to worry about. I was more concerned about the damage the snipers could do to us in the open gun pits. I would have been much more concerned had I known then what I learned later. The small-arms fire was not coming from snipers, but from the first wave of assault troops no more than fifty meters outside the perimeter.

After what seemed like an eternity, the mortars stopped falling.

I'm sure no one was counting, but the official after-action reports listed the incoming as a barrage of over three hundred rounds. I can assure you, I wouldn't argue over a higher number.

The silence was not to last very long. Within seconds, the sounds of hundreds of AK-47s, machine guns, RPGs, and grenades shattered the quiet surrounding our perimeter. The ground assault had began.

The VC's main assault was from the north and northeast, directed at Charlie Company's portion of the perimeter. The volume of fire, from both the VC and our return fire, was mind-boggling.

We shifted both guns to the northeast and dropped the range to two hundred meters. We didn't have time to plot the data and lay the guns: We used good ole Kentucky windage, and it worked. We could see the flash when the rounds exploded and made minor adjustments to the tube.

We could see the wave of VC moving toward the perimeter across the open field, as they were silhouetted by the explosions.

All sense of time was lost. There were only four or five rounds left out of thirty-five, in our gun position. Probably there were about the same in Snake's. The VC had managed to reach the perimeter at one point in Charlie Company's sector. I could see them firing toward the bunkers they had just left as they pulled back. I remember pointing out the break in the perimeter to Sergeant West and telling him to fire everything he had left in front of that area.

I jumped out of the gun pit and made a dash for Snake's pit. Right before I got to the pit, I stepped on an empty mortar canister, went sailing through the air and landed flat on my back. I remember the first thing I thought was *My God, I'm hit!* When I tried to move and couldn't, I knew I had been hit and was paralyzed.

That's when I had my second talk that morning with God.

I had only strained my back and had the wind knocked out of me, but I didn't know that. I was sure I had just become a statistic for the 5:30 newscasts back home.

My memory of what actually happened during the next few minutes is a bit hazy. I know there was a lot of movement in and around our position, as members of my company and Alpha Company moved to reestablish the perimeter, and the wounded from Charlie Company were being brought over to our area.

I found myself in Snake's gun pit when my senses returned. We were finally getting some artillery fire, and the volume of incoming fire had died down. I had just started feeling good about the artillery when the VC increased their rate of fire. I looked out over the sandbags of the pit and saw another wave of VC beginning their onslaught of the perimeter. They were so close we couldn't fire our M16s for fear of hitting our own men moving into position to counter the attack.

At that moment I remember looking up and seeing the most beautiful sight I have ever seen. The gray clouds had broken up and the blue sky was visible. The jets that had been circling over the area, waiting for a break in the clouds, were coming in.

They dropped napalm and CBUs on their first pass, about one hundred yards out from the perimeter. Their next pass was closer in. One jet screamed in at treetop level on our side of the perimeter and dropped CBUs no more than fifty meters from the gun pit. We stood up and cheered as if we were at a football game.

After countless runs to our front and flanks, the jets continued to strike to the north as they followed the retreating VC.

After four long, ungodly hours, we could finally stand up and breathe a sigh of relief. Our battle was over. That's when I had my third talk of the morning with God.

I grabbed Snake in a bear hug and noticed his face for the first time. It was puffed up and looked like somebody had tried to put his head in a waffle iron. He had fired his last few rounds with the tube almost straight up. His hands were wrapped with his shirt but the hot tube slipped and hit his face. Although he would have scars for a while, he was smiling from ear to ear. I saw why when I looked down. Lying next to the mortar were two dud chicom grenades.

Walking around our position was like being in a dream world—a bad dream. Charlie Company was using Sergeant West's gun pit and the FDC bunker for an aid station for the wounded. Dust-offs were lined up in the

LZ just outside our positions. The entire area in front of our fighting positions was covered with dead VC. Most of the bodies had fresh bandages over wounds received during their first assault. Some were still whole, many were in pieces, thanks to the artillery and air strikes. Still hanging from a tree with his telephone swinging from a limb was the remains of the FO that had adjusted the VC mortar fire. The acrid smell of cordite was overwhelming.

The DePuy Fighting Position had, without a doubt, proved itself to any and all skeptics under the most trying conditions. Without them, the mortar barrage alone would have wiped us out.

I still refer to artillerymen as "lanyard yankers," and joke about the "fly boys" of the air force, but I also give credit where credit is due. In the short time span of some eighteen hours, the artillery fired over 15,000 rounds in our support; the air force flew 133 sorties in our defense. There is no doubt in my mind that without their support, I would not be sitting here telling my story today.

To say that we were outnumbered during the battle would be more than an understatement of the facts. The official reports listed the strength of the 271st VC Regiment at 2500 regulars. When the smoke cleared over the battlefield, the VC had left 609 dead soldiers on or near our perimeter. God only knows how many more were wounded and died later. For all practical purposes, the 9th VC Division had been wiped out in a little over three weeks during Operation Junction City.

Our battalion casualties were listed as ten killed in action and sixty-four wounded. There were no casualties in my platoon.

We were air lifted out of LZ George sometime before noon and taken to Quan Loi. That was the best chopper ride I'd ever had.

General Westmoreland flew in to congratulate the

battalion for a job well done. That's when we were told that LTC Haig had been promoted to colonel and was the new 2d Brigade commander.

After we were resupplied, we got a much-needed and well-deserved rest before moving back to Phuoc Vinh. The afternoon was for letter writing—some short notes to girl friends, many long letters to the family, but all were thankful.

Chapter 15

HOME

WE SPENT THE NEXT FEW WEEKS CONDUCTING LOCAL SECURITY and sweep operations in and around Phuoc Vinh. We also spent a lot of time as a rapid reaction force, sitting around the airstrip prepared for eagle flights. We were slowly getting new replacements in and the company strength was edging up. Even after Reb and Killer had left for the "land of the big PX," the platoon strength had climbed all the way up to twenty.

After months of scrounging for material and working when the time was available, the battalion NCO club was completed and opened. It was a medium-sized tropical hootch and provided ample space for the NCOs of the battalion. We had to substitute a small stereo system for a juke box, but it served the purpose and was just as good. It didn't open until after the evening meal was served in the mess hall, about 1700 hours (5:00 P.M.). The music always started out with some hot rock-and-roll records, but after a few beers the tempo seemed to slow down to more somber ballads. One record, "I Want To Go Home," had been played so much you had to strain to hear it. Even that didn't present a problem. By the time everybody joined in the singing, you couldn't hear the record anyway.

★　★　★　★

Somewhere around the middle of May, I was flown to Long Binh and reported to a general officer I had known and worked for while assigned to the 3rd Infantry Division in Germany. He was assigned to Headquarters, USARV. I had met him in the field once during a bridge security operation when a lot of brass came out for a briefing, and we had discussed old times.

I had been the coach of the 1st Brigade's baseball team, the "Crusaders," in 1965. We beat everybody in Germany and France that year, and were the 3rd Division champions. Our record was something like thirty-two wins and two losses.

The general, who was a brigade commander at the time, was an avid baseball fan and gave us all the support one could ever ask for. A good example is the fact that we never had a home game called because of a wet field; the colonel would send a helicopter over to the field an hour or two before game time to "blow dry" the field. On more than one occasion, he appeared in the dugout prior to the start of a game, and "ordered" us to win because he had a nice sum of money riding on us. I'm sure he more than made up for our two losses that year.

He told me there was a job for an operations sergeant open in a unit in Saigon. The unit handled all logistical and support elements assigned to Saigon. He asked me if I wanted the job.

What did a young staff sergeant say to a general who was offering him a ticket out of the dreaded boonies? With deep gratitude, I answered yes and thanked him.

Within a week, I received orders assigning me to Headquarters Detachment, USAHAC.

I left Phuoc Vinh and the Blue Spaders with mixed emotions. Sure, I was glad to know that I wouldn't have to face the unknown of the jungle any longer. I knew I wouldn't miss the stifling heat, nor the long marches with the constant fear that my next step could be the last one I took. I could live without the sweaty palms, the dry mouth, and the sudden rapid increase of heartbeat caused by the sound of an AK-47 fired in my direction. The absence of all those things, although never forgotten, would be more than welcome.

On the other hand, I felt badly about the fact that I was leaving my men, who would continue living with those dangers and fears, day in and day out. I guess the simplest way to put it is I felt guilty.

It's hard to explain the bond that develops between men engaged in combat to someone who hasn't been a part of a combat unit. I guess the best way to express the feeling is by a comparison of the family. A mother, father, sons, and daughters live, eat, sleep, and face the problems of coping in society and together for many years. Most of the time they coexist as one, a single unit.

Place a small group of men who differ in age, race, and background together; require that they eat, sleep, work, and play as one, every minute of the day for a period of many months. Add to this the fear of possible death at the hands of the enemy at any moment and you have a situation much more trying and demanding than that of the family unit. Your feelings become those of the group. You share the happy times and feel their sadness as much as they do. Everyone realizes the importance of doing his job to the best of his ability to insure the others' safety.

A strong bond, almost like love, develops between these warriors and lives forever. You can see evidence of this at reunions when old veterans gather to relive past hardships and experiences. You can feel and see these men have something very special in common. Their faces glow as they embrace; the pride expands their chests; and eyes grow watery as they remember the ones not present.

It's almost like a family reunion, but somehow even closer.

I left Phuoc Vinh, and the men I had grown to love, with tears in my eyes.

For the next four months, before going back to the "world," I was to become a "Saigon Warrior," the much-hated REMF.

But that's another story.

★ ★ ★ ★

My eyes were glued to the big shiny airliner sitting next to the terminal at Bien Hoa Air Force Base. Earlier, I had watched as the plane had taxied up to the terminal and its cargo of new soldiers filed down the steps to be greeted by the heat. I remembered how I felt when I stepped off a plane like that a lifetime ago. I thought how ironic it was that we who were preparing to leave would call this plane a "Freedom Bird," when it had just brought over two hundred soldiers into the same place we felt lucky to be leaving.

I watched the plane for over an hour as it was refueled and our baggage was loaded. I felt as if I was protecting the plane from any harm or damage as long as I watched. I could imagine the VC launching a rocket or mortar attack and destroying the big beautiful jet even as we taxied to takeoff position.

The flight crew welcomed us aboard shortly before nightfall and helped make us comfortable. The air conditioning aboard the plane was welcome, but we were all asking for blankets before long. The expressions on the faces of my fellow passengers seemed to be frozen somewhere between relief and sheer ecstasy. There wasn't very much talking or noise as we taxied to our takeoff position. A group of eight or nine young soldiers sporting new corporal and sergeant stripes were generating what little noise there was. They had obviously started celebrating their departure before getting on the plane. Except for the noise generated by the jet engines, it was very quiet as the plane hurled down the runway. A tremendous roar filled the plane when we felt the wheels lift off the runway and the nose shot up in a sharp climb to gain altitude. The expressions on the faces were different now. The nervous stares had been replaced with those of elation and relief. Although army regulations prohibited the airline from serving alcoholic beverages during the flight, an ample supply of bottles had been smuggled aboard to permit everyone a toast.

A short time later, the captain made an announcement that called for renewed cheers and another toast. We had just cleared the air space of South Vietnam.

Two days later, I was back home with my parents and son in Alabama. But the "world" I had known before going to Vietnam had changed. College students were beginning to protest our involvement in Vietnam, draft cards were being burnt at protest rallies, and the sight of a soldier in uniform hushed conversations and drew stares of disapproval. People once referred to as friends were no longer friendly. The politicians seemed to be encouraging the split in our nation by taking every possible measure to fight recommendations of our military leaders.

It should have come as no surprise that the young returning GIs, only two or three days out of the madness of combat, were puzzled by this cold reception. They didn't expect or want everyone in New York to turn out for a ticker tape parade, as they had when Johnny came marching home from over there. We didn't return home as a unit, like they did. We came back as individuals to face our dreams and nightmares alone. There were many sleepless nights and nights of waking up in a cold sweat, screaming. For some it was too much, for others the nightmares still occur. The only thing we expected from our nation was that our services and accomplishments be recognized and appreciated, nothing more.

I spent about two weeks with my family, visiting relatives and friends, and eating everything in sight that wasn't in a tin can!

My next assignment was as an instructor at The Citadel, in Charleston, South Carolina.

The highest compliment a teacher can ever receive from a former student comes in the form of two words—*thank you*. I have had the pleasure of that experience many times.

In May 1969, I voluntarily returned for a second tour of duty in Vietnam with the 1st Infantry Division. In April 1970, I had the honor of returning the Division's colors to Fort Riley, Kansas, upon their withdrawal from Vietnam.

These memories are forever.

Chapter 16

AFTERTHOUGHTS

WHEN I WAS A YOUNG BUCK SERGEANT, I gazed in awe whenever I saw a senior NCO or officer wearing the blue-and-silver wreath-encircled rifle above his left pocket. The Combat Infantryman's Badge boldly stated that the wearer was a member of an elite group of men that had seen, and lived through, all the hell and hardships of combat. They had experienced first hand the fear of not seeing the next sunrise, the unforgettable smell of cordite after a battle, and had cradled in their arms the bloody, mangled lifeless form of what was only seconds before their best buddy.

These men had served during the Korean conflict and, a few, during the "big war," WW II—the "Good War." Their service was during an "honorable" period. They endured their hardships and were welcomed home with praises and parades by a grateful nation. They wore their badge of courage with pride.

That generation has been replaced today by my generation—the unpopular era of Vietnam. The one always referred to as "the one we lost." Will the young NCOs of tomorrow still respect that little badge of courage? I sure hope so. For although the welcomes and parades have been a long time in coming, the CIB means the same today and is still worn with pride by those of us who returned.

★　★　★　★

Ten thousand miles (give or take a few) is a long way to travel, even under the best of circumstances.

In late December 1966, I was granted an emergency leave to get home and start divorce proceedings to fight another battle for the right to keep my son.

I remembered the twenty-hour flight from California—my God, it had only been a little over two months, and it seemed as if I had lived half a lifetime during that short span! I knew the flight back to Alabama would be a long one.

I arrived at Bien Hoa Air Base with mixed emotions. Word of the divorce came as a complete shock to me and I, naturally, was feeling sorry for myself. At the same time, I felt guilty for leaving my men, even for a couple of weeks. Here I was going back to civilization, back to "the world," but there was no joy or happiness to be found in the fact.

I had been at the terminal only a short time when I was paged to report to the departure desk. The air force sergeant explained it would be another twelve hours before the next scheduled transport plane departed.

"You can get a bunk over at the BEQ and sack out for a while, or you can get a hop on a C-141 going to Travis Air Force Base in about twenty minutes. It's loaded with cargo and not set up for passengers, but I think the crew would set up a sling seat for you. Let me check with the flight commander."

He got on the phone and looked back up at me after a minute.

"The captain says it's okay with him if you don't mind the inconvenience."

I told him it would be fine with me. I didn't really want to wait any longer than I had to.

He showed me to a jeep that took me to the big cargo

plane and I boarded just as the rear of the ship was being closed.

I was shown to a sling seat at the front of the long cargo area by the crew chief. He told me to make myself as comfortable as possible and brought me a blanket. It was already cool, and we were still sitting on the ground. He managed to tell me as the engines roared to life that the cargo was off limits and to use the front latrine when I had to go.

I looked down the length of the large cargo plane as we taxied to take off position. The center of the cargo area was stacked with long metal crates secured by OD nylon rigging straps. There were two rows of six on the bottom and the same number stacked on top, a total of twenty-four.

We had gained our cruising altitude and leveled off before I realized what the cargo was. I wasn't the only passenger on this flight, as I had thought when I boarded; but I was by far the luckiest. The large metal crates contained the bodies of twenty-four men who weren't so lucky. They were going home too, but not the way they had dreamed or planned to.

I quickly realized how small my problems really were. I couldn't find any room in my mind to feel sorry for myself now.

It was a long trip to California. I caught another C-141 out of Travis that was going all the way to Maxwell AFB in Montgomery, Alabama, my home. This plane was equipped for passengers and a little more comfortable. But every time I looked down the long aisle, I saw the twenty-four long metal crates.

If I boarded a plane even today, I'm sure I would still see them. But for the grace of God, one of them could have been mine.

"Dear Mrs. Swinney . . . " With those three words, I started the longest and most difficult letter I have ever had to write.

It was the afternoon of 1 April 1967. We had been air lifted out of Ap Gu to Quan Loi to get resupplied and have a chance to settle our nerves. This day had already seemed like the longest day in history. I know I aged more than one day.

The letter wasn't long lengthwise, it was only one hand-written page; it was long because it was so difficult to find the right words to express my feelings. It's not very easy to tell a young pregnant wife of only a few months that her husband won't be coming home. He would never get to see or hold the baby he talked so much about, or hold his wife the way he had in all his dreams.

It wasn't easy, but I felt it was my responsibility. I didn't have to write her and tell her the bad news. I could have done nothing and she would have been notified by a cold, formal letter signed by some total stranger in Washington. A young officer probably from Fort Knox would be assigned as Survivors Assistance Officer to help her with funeral arrangements and taking care of all the necessary legal papers. He, too, would have been a total stranger to the family.

Joe and I were very close, and I knew he had mentioned me in his many letters home. He always shared parts of his letters with us, and I didn't consider myself a stranger even though I had never met his wife or family.

I tried to be as up-beat as I could (if that is even possible under those circumstances); there was nothing to hide or play down, because Joe had always been an exceptional soldier and an asset to the platoon. I told her

I considered Joe as my brother, the brother I never had. I told her the truth and prayed that she wouldn't hold me responsible (even though I was) for his death. It was almost dark when I finished the letter and I had to hustle to finish a letter to my folks before it grew too dark beneath the rubber trees to see.

About three weeks later I received a small note postmarked in Tennessee. Mrs. Swinney thanked me for telling her about Joe, and I knew the longest letter I had ever written had been worth the time and pain it took to write.

I still have that dirt-smudged little note to this day.

★   ★   ★   ★

A lot of thoughts go through your head when you're in a mortar pit with shrapnel and bullets whizzing past your ears. The angry, hornetlike sounds of an AK-47 round that misses your head by inches convinces you that all the time spent on digging the mortars in was well worthwhile. If you have any second thoughts at all, it would be that of deserving a swift kick in the butt for not going another two or three inches deeper, or adding another row of sandbags on top.

One thought that does not enter your mind is that of doing something heroic or trying to emulate one of John Wayne's stunts. Those things look good in the movies because we have grown to expect them from stars like John Wayne, Lee Marvin, Aldo Ray, and Sly Stallone. But nobody is firing real bullets at them.

We've all read articles and heard individuals relate their experiences after a near-fatal incident. Some tell how in a matter of seconds, their whole life flashed before their eyes. Believe me, it's true. It's almost like a VCR on fast forward, except much faster. Memories from your younger days, your mom and dad, your wife and kids, even that special car back home: everything that you hold dear quickly flashes before your mind's eye. Just as quickly it is gone, and once again reality sets in.

Quite naturally, survival becomes the uppermost thing on your mind, both yours and your men's.

With adrenalin rushing through our veins, we react to the situation without consciously thinking about what we are doing. Our actions during this period must be credited not only to our prior training and instincts, but also to plain old fear.

When the danger is over and we calm down, we often have no idea what actions we took. We know we survived, and we got from point A to point B, but we don't have the foggiest idea what took place in between.

Looking back through history, we would have fewer heroes today if someone had not witnessed the actions of a person who was reacting to fear.

If a Vietnam veteran says he was never afraid or never knew fear while engaged in a fire fight, he is either a liar or has never been in a fire fight.

★   ★   ★   ★

They say time flies when you're having fun. I must have been having a lot of fun during the past nineteen or so years because time has really flown by.

Looking back, I realize I have had a lot of fun and much good fortune. I met and married a wonderful girl from Alabama, who became a mother to my son and a perfect wife to me. We have had the privilege of traveling to and living in some fantastic places like Charleston, South Carolina and Hawaii. We have been blessed with the opportunity to meet and make many friends like Pat and Bill Kemmitt, Glo and Dwayne Aaron, and Alma and Don Jones, just to name a few. We've never been rich or had enough money (who has?) but we haven't gone hungry either, and the life we've shared has been full of love. We have a lot to be thankful for, because the years have been so full. I'm sure I can't remember all the good times we've shared these past years.

Yet, when two or three Vietnam vets meet and begin swapping "war stories," all the years seem to vanish. The revived memories of events that took place twenty years before, suddenly seem to have happened only yesterday, or a week ago at the most. We have little or no trouble recalling the names and faces of men in our unit, but discover we have difficulty trying to remember the name of a co-worker just five years ago.

★   ★   ★   ★

General Sherman, of Civil War fame, coined a phrase that has been repeated many times: War is hell. I couldn't agree more.

If God had created a place worse than hell, I would not hesitate to precede it with "Guerrilla war is . . ."

It's bad enough when you know where the enemy has his camps, what their strength is, and what armament they are equipped with.

The force that finds itself fighting a guerrilla war has to start from scratch at the very beginning. There are no clearly defined front lines for the tacticians to neatly plot on their big war maps. There is no such thing as enemy-held terrain and friendly territory. The enemy does not even wear a distinctive military uniform.

The base camp of a guerrilla force might be the little village right next to your base camp. They are not very concerned about holding terrain. The very nature of guerrilla warfare tactics stresses the importance of disrupting lines of communications and being highly mobile.

Guerrilla force members come in all sizes, from a five-year-old child to a fifty-year-old mama-san. The female workers in your mess hall, listening to conversations about future operations, alert local guerrillas and many times participate in the ambush of your unit. The barber that you trust to cut your hair and shave you tries to kill you by lobbing rocket and mortar rounds into your base camp at night. The mama-san and papa-san that smile and wave at you as you pass them working in their field could be members of the guerrilla force that hits your perimeter that night. The small five- or six-year-old child with the big brown, pleading eyes who was begging for "chop-chop" yesterday might drop a grenade at your feet today. The mother of the child is around the corner smiling, as she sells you an ice-cold Coke with finely ground glass in the bottom.

All of these examples, and many more, were repeated hundreds of times throughout Vietnam. How do you know who the enemy is? How can you tell, before it's too late?

Guerrilla war is . . .

★ ★ ★ ★

The last thing I want is to leave the impression that I am glorifying war. War is the most horrible thing that can happen to God's creation. The death of hundreds of thousands of bright young men and women cannot be justified by any amount of reasoning.

The purpose of a well-equipped, well-trained fighting force is to project a strong deterrent. A good soldier will be the first to tell you that he hopes he never has to experience combat, because he knows better than anyone the terrible consequences that are possible. But when we are involved in a conflict, we who are trained to handle the situation must be prepared and ready to serve.

I went back to Vietnam because I felt that was where I should be. My training and experience could best be utilized back in the jungle. I was confident my knowledge would help save a few lives.

I gained that confidence largely through association with other confident people. Good units don't just happen; they are created and perpetuated by a lot of hard work, dedication, and excellent leadership. One weak link in a chain ruins the effectiveness of the entire chain.

The people I was privileged to work with made a lasting impression on my life. People like General Haig, General DePuy, and General Rogers were the epitome of excellence, and the chain didn't get any weaker down the links, Captain Simms, Lieutenant DeVane, 1SG Webb, Killer, and Snake, all the way to the last link, the PFC that eargerly carried the heavy mortar rounds on his back through the jungles. They all played a big part in my education.

There is no acceptable substitute for excellence; without it you can only have failure.

GLOSSARY

AO—Military abbreviation for *Area of Operations*

APC—Armored Personnel Carrier. Means of transportation for mechanized units.

A-RATIONS—Real, cooked food.

BATTA BOOTS—A bootlike tennis shoe worn by the enemy and some ARVN units.

BDA—Bomb Damage Assessment. A report on the damage caused by an air strike.

BOONIES—A term used to describe the jungle.

BOONIE RATS—The term used to describe infantry troops.

CBU—Type of bomb. A group of small bombs in a pod that scatters over the area before exploding.

C & C—Command and Control. Term used to describe a commander's helicopter.

CHIEU HOI—Term used by VC to surrender under the government's "Open Arms" program.

CHINOOK—The large, twin-rotor helicopter used to transport heavy equipment and artillery. Sometimes referred to as a "shit-hook."

COBRA—Assault gun ships.

COSVN—Communist Central Office of South Vietnam. It was reportedly never found, but I think we got pretty close in April 1967.

C-RATS—Combat rations. Processed, canned food that took a good imagination to eat.

DAISY CUTTER—10,000-pound bomb. One of its uses was that of clearing trees in the preparation of an LZ or position.

DEFCON—Artillery term for defensive concentration.

DUST-OFF—Term given to the medical evacuation choppers and crewmen.

143

DUSTER—Term for the twin forty-millimeter air-defense artillery guns mounted on an APC chassis.

FDC—Fire Direction Center. The brain center where artillery and mortar data is computed and sent to the guns for firing.

FSB—Fire support base. The location of one or more artillery units providing fires for infantry units.

FAST MOVER—An F-4 jet.

FO—Forward Observer. The artillery's representative attached to the infantry unit to call for and adjust artillery or mortar fires.

GOOK—Term used to describe the enemy. Also, "dink," "slope," and "slant-eye."

GRUNT—Nickname for the infantry soldier.

GUNSHIP—Cobra or huey slick with rocket pods and mounted machine guns.

HE—Abbreviation for a type of shell: High Explosive.

H & I—Harassment and Interdiction. A preplanned artillery or mortar target, fired at random times during the night.

HO CHI MINH SANDALS—Footwear used by the VC made from the rubber of tires.

HOT LZ—A term used to describe a landing zone when enemy fire is expected or being received.

IRON TRIANGLE—An area bounded by the village of Ben Suc, Ben Cat, and Phu Cong in our AO. A known VC stronghold. A large portion was destroyed by Rome Plows during Operation Cedar Falls.

LP—Listening Post.

LZ—Landing Zone.

LZ PREP—The "softening" of an LZ by artillery and air prior to an insertion.

MPC—Military Payment Certificate. Also "funny money."

MR. CHARLES—A more respectful nickname for the cunning VC.

NAPALM—A thick mixture that burst into an engulfing flame upon exploding. Dropped in a canister by jets.

NDP—Night Defensive Position.

NUMBA 1—Phrase used by the Vietnamese to describe the best.

NUMBA 10—Phrase used to describe something bad.

NVA—North Vietnamese Army regulars.

PZ—Pick-up Zone.

POINT—Position at the very front of a formation during movement. A very important and dangerous job.

PUFF—C-47 aircraft equipped with miniguns capable of firing 6,000 rounds per minute. Also dropped flares that lit up the entire battle area. Also called "Spooky."

ROME PLOW—An engineer vehicle equipped with a large cutting blade. Used in jungle clearing operations.

RFPF—South Vietnamese Regional Forces and Popular Forces. Called the "Ruff-Puffs." Served as local area defensive forces.

SAIGON WARRIOR—The grunts' term for GIs assigned plush jobs in Saigon.

SAIGON TEA—Non-alcoholic beverage bought for the bar girls by GIs.

SLICK—Term used to describe an unarmed huey chopper used for supply runs and transporting grunts.

USAHAC—United States Army Headquarters Area Command.

USARV—United States Army Vietnam.

WD-1—Communications wire.